SHAHROKH MESKOOB

Iranian National Identity and the Persian Language

Foreword with Author Interview by Ali Banuazizi

Translated by Michael C. Hillmann

Edited by John R. Perry

MAGE PUBLISHERS
WASHINGTON, D.C.

Mage and colophon are registered trademarks of Mage Publishers, Inc.

Manufactured in the United States of America

Library of Congress Cataloging-in-Publication Data

Nationality and Language / by Shahrokh Meskoob ;
translated by Michael Hillmann ; edited by John Perry;
introduction by Ali Banuazizi

p. cm.

Translation of: Melliyat va zaban

1. Persian language—History. 2. Persian language—Religious aspects—Islam.
3. Language policy—Iran—History.
I. Hillmann, Michael C. II. Title

PK10225.M413 1992

491'.55'09—dc20

Print on Demand Edition
ISBN: 978-1-933823-81-2

www.mage.com
as@mage.com

Roles of the Court, Religion, and Sufism in Persian Prose Writing

Contents

Foreword

Ali Banuazizi

What comprises the Iranians' sense of "Iranianness"—that unique amalgam of shared history, religion(s), language(s), myths, artistic expression, sentiments, and traditions that has provided them with an enduring and resilient cultural identity as members of one of the world's oldest civilizations? How widely—and deeply—is such an identity shared by the various ethnolinguistic groups that live within the boundaries of the present Iranian state and by those in Afghanistan, Central Asia, and the Caucasus who share their language and much of their cultural heritage with Iranians? And how variable has been this identity in the various periods of Iran's cultural history? While these questions are certainly not new, they have gained much greater significance with the political upheavals that followed the Iranian Revolution of 1979, the initial efforts of the Revolution's clerical leadership to forge a new cultural identity for Iranians as an "Islamic nation," and, more recently, the surge of ethnic assertiveness and conflict in several of Iran's neighboring states in Central and Southwest Asia.

Of the various elements that constitute Iran's cultural identity, four have traditionally been judged the most salient. These include: (1) the country's pre-Islamic legacy, which took shape over a period of more

than a millennium, from the time of Achaemenians to the defeat of the
last Persian dynasty (the Sasanians) by the invading Arab armies in the
middle of the seventh century; (2) Islam, or, more specifically, Shi'ism,
the religion of over 90 percent of the country's present-day inhabitants,
with an all-encompassing impact on every facet of Iranian culture and
thought; (3) the more diffuse bonds, fictive or real, established among
peoples who have inhabited roughly the same territory, with the same
name, faced the same enemies, struggled under the same despotic rulers
and conquerors, and otherwise shared the same historical destiny for
over two millennia; and finally (4) the Persian language, currently the
mother tongue of a bare majority of the population, but long the literary
and "national language" in Iran (as well as in parts of Afghanistan,
Central Asia, and the Indian subcontinent). The relative weight to be
given to each of these partially overlapping elements in defining the
Iranian national identity has generated much controversy among the
successive generations of modern intellectuals in Iran, particularly since
the last decades of the nineteenth century, when the question of national
identity moved to the center stage of the political discourse.

The focus of the present work by Shahrokh Meskoob, one of Iran's
leading contemporary authors and cultural historians, is on the last of
the above elements—i. e., the Persian language—and its role in forming
and sustaining the Iranian national identity. The author stresses the fact
that following the Arab conquest of Persia in the seventh century C.E.,
it took Persians well over two centuries to recover from their humiliating
defeat, a defeat which entailed not only the crumbling of their political
order and subjugation to foreign rule, but also the imposition of a new
religion and language on them. In the struggle to regain their cultural
identity as a separate people, their most important recourse was their
pre-Islamic history, as remembered, imagined, and reconstructed, for
the most part, in the mytho-historical narratives, "books of kings" (the
shahnamehs) composed in this period, of which Ferdowsi's *Shahnameh*
(1010 C.E.) is the preeminent example. The use of Persian in these and
other works gradually established it as the principal literary language
and, as such, the feature that most distinguished the Iranians from the
rest of the Islamic world. In Meskoob's words, "Only with respect to two
things were we Iranians separate from other Muslims: history and
language, the two factors on which we proceeded to build our own
identity as a people or nation. History was our currency, the provisions
for the way, and our refuge. Language was the foundation, floor, and
refuge for the soul, a stronghold within which we stood" (p. 13). This

reclaiming of cultural identity by the Persians, it must be emphasized, however, never acquired the character of an anti-Islamic impulse. Indeed, the acceptance of Persian as the second language of Islam brought to it a certain measure of sanctity. The increasing acceptance and use of Persian, especially in its written form, in the Iranian world as the principal language for formal communication and literary expression served as one—if not the key—link among the many peoples that comprised the Iranian civilization.

The core of Meskoob's book is his assessment, through a careful review of hundreds of literary, religious, and mystical works by Persian-speaking authors from the tenth to the end of the nineteenth century, of the role of three major social groups—the courtiers and bureaucratic officials, the religious scholars (the *ulama*), and the Muslim mystics (the Sufis) in the spread and flourishing of Persian in the Iranian cultural world. Of the three groups, he finds the *ulama* contributed the least to the development of Persian; the most eminent among them preferred to write in Arabic, and their use of Persian was mostly for purposes of oral communication with the masses. The two groups that served as the "guardians" of the language and helped in its flourishing and further refinement as a major literary, diplomatic, and administrative language in Iran and elsewhere were the Muslim Gnostics (the Sufi poets and writers) and those in the employ of the royal court and state-bureaucratic apparatus (*ahl-e divan*).

It is precisely this emphasis on the role of particular social groups in the development of the Persian language and literature that sets Meskoob's analysis apart from the more conventional approaches to Persian literary history as pursued, for example, in the works of Edward G. Browne, Jan Rypka, and Zabihollâh Safa. Where the latter authors followed a chronological approach to the development of Persian literature in relation to its general historical and cultural contexts, Meskoob seeks to show how the particular sociocultural positions held by the aforementioned groups helped determine the nature and extent of their respective contributions to the development of the Persian language. His study, therefore, offers an excellent example of a sociologically sensitive analysis of Iranian cultural history and identity.

Meskoob's examination of the role of the Persian language in the formation and continuity of Iranian identity ends with the Constitutional Movement of 1905–11. He maintains that with the political and social changes that took place in the closing decades of the nineteenth century, and with Persia's increasing contact with the West, the three social groups on which his analysis is focused lost their significance as the principal guardians, practitioners, and promoters of the Persian language. In all these capacities they were gradually replaced by a new social group in the Iranian society, i.e., a secular intelligentsia consisting of journalists, writers, poets, etc. An analysis of their role vis-á-vis the Persian language, and in relation to the masses and the state, as the author rightly points out, lies beyond the scope of the present work.

Aside from his deep knowledge of cultural history, what the author brings to his survey of the evolution of the Persian language and its relation to the Iranian national identity are his insights and skills as one of Iran's foremost literary critics. His own masterful use of the Persian language, his interpretive works on Persia's most celebrated classical poets (Ferdowsi and Hafez), and numerous other translations, literary and philosophical essays, and short stories give special authority to his views on what is undoubtedly one of the most difficult problems in Iranian intellectual history.* We are also very fortunate to have had Michael Hillmann, one of the leading scholars of Persian literature in the United States, translate this work into English with extensive notations that clearly enhance its value and usefulness to the English reader.

---

*Shahrokh Meskoob's major published works include translations of Sophocles' *Antigone, Oedipus Rex, and Oedipus at Colonus*, reissued as *Afsaneha-ye Tebai* (Tehran: Entesharat-e Kharazmi, 1352 [1973]); *Moqaddame-'i bar Rostam va Esfandiar* [a study of the ethics of Ferdowsi's Shahnameh] (Tehran: Ketabha-ye Jibi, 1342 [1963]); *Soug-e Siavosh* [a study of the myth of martyrdom and resurrection in the Shahnameh](Tehran: Entesharat-e Kharazmi, 1350 [1971]); and *Dar kuy-e dust* [an interpretive study of Hafez's views on man, nature, love, and ethics] (Tehran: Entesharat-e Kharazmi, 1357 [1978]). The original Persian edition of the present work was first published under the title of *Melliyat va zaban* (Paris, 1982).

An Interview with Shahrokh Meskoob

The following interview, part of a more wide-ranging series of interviews with Shahrokh Meskoob, was conducted on March 25, 1989 in Boston. It was translated from the Persian and slightly edited by Ali Banuazizi for the present volume.

Ali Banuazizi: Let me begin by asking you about the circumstances under which the lectures upon which this book is based were given, and your state of mind at that time.

Shahrokh Meskoob: I gave these talks, spread over ten or so sessions, in the late spring and early summer of 1981, a little over two years after the revolution. The state of mind of the Iranian exile community living in Paris at that time is not difficult to imagine. Many of the intellectuals who had left Iran during or shortly after the revolution were experiencing a sense of disorientation and shock. They were much more inclined in those days to get together and talk about what had happened to them and to their country. I was asked to participate in a lecture series that had included talks by Nader Naderpour on Iran's major classical poets and by Mohammad Ja'far Mahjoub on Iranian folk literature. The lectures were given at the Pierre Brosselette School in Paris, where the Iranian poet Yadollah Roya'i had organized Persian-language classes for elementary and secondary school students {Persian had been recognized as a second language by the French educational authorities}. My lectures were third in this series, and I had been asked to discuss topics dealing with language and literature. As the lectures progressed, however, certain ideas nascent in my mind began to crystallize and come to focus. My thinking gradually shifted from specific literary issues to the problem of the Iranian national identity and the role played by Persian history and language in its formation during the third to the fifth Islamic centuries [ninth to eleventh centuries C.E.]. I had initially prepared some notes for what I thought would be a series of no more than two or three lectures, but it quickly became apparent that the topic was too complex to be dealt with so briefly. I expanded the talks, but at the time I had no intention of having them appear in print. However, after seeing the transcripts, I thought that it might be worthwhile to do so, and so I went over the transcripts, added a few notes, rewrote a few pages, and had them published in Paris in 1982.

AB: Do you think that your own reaction to the Iranian revolution and your decision to leave the country and live in exile in France had much of an impact on the tone and content of the lectures—the whole emphasis on the theme of identity, for example?

SM: The concern with the question of identity did not begin with my leaving Iran. From the time that I was in the seventh or eighth grade, I developed a strong interest in Persian classical literature. In fact, I would say that increasingly Persian poetry and prose, and later, the *Shahnameh*, became the very cornerstones of my thinking and sense of personal identity. After the 1979 revolution and the many attacks on Persian language, literature, and, in particular, on Ferdowsi by several prominent members of the new regime, my concern with the problem of cultural identity became much more than a personal preoccupation. What was being attacked, I felt, was something that belonged to an entire society. Our whole sense of identity as a people and a nation, I thought, was in jeopardy. I don't have that fear anymore.

In Paris, I think the intellectual aspects of the problem began to interest me more. In other words, after the emotional pain and turmoil that I had experienced in Iran, I could move some distance from the problem and reflect on it more objectively. Perhaps this would not have happened if I had remained in Iran.

AB: It seems that your experience of exile was quite different, then, from that of people like the late Gholamhossein Sa'edi, who was also very much concerned with the fate of culture in Iran after the revolution. For him, as you know, life in exile was filled with frustration and anguish.

SM: I think our problems were quite different. I never experienced the feeling of estrangement in Paris that he did. In Iran, a good deal of my interest and attention was focused on the West. After coming to Europe, however, I became more preoccupied with Iran—in a sense, I have "lived" much more in Iran since leaving it than I did when I was there. But all this has been more at the intellectual rather than the emotional level.

AB: As I recall, you were in fact among the small minority of intellectuals in Iran who, in the years leading to the revolution, did not participate in the fashionable *gharb-setizi* movement—i. e., the ideological crusade against the West and its culture that was spearheaded by Al-e Ahmad, Shari'ati, and Naraqi, among others.

SM: No. In fact, at about the time that that movement was at its height I was struggling with Lukacs's *Theory of the Novel*. I had a great deal of difficulty understanding the book the first time I read it. It was the first book that I began to reread the moment I finished it; even after the second reading I could only understand bits and pieces of it because I was not familiar with some of the basic elements of his argument. But each passage that I understood opened a new window, revealed a new literary insight for me.

With regard to the anti-Western climate of those prerevolutionary days, I recall a meeting at the Plan Organization with the Undersecretary for Planning, the Minister of Culture and the Arts (one of the "official" promoters of the campaign against the West), the head of the High Council on Culture and the Arts, and several others. I was attending the meeting as a staff member of the Cultural Planning Bureau of the Plan Organization. After listening to their many laments and attacks on the ills of the West, I could no longer contain myself and said, "I think we Iranians are, on the whole, culturally lazy. Although we have had dealings with the Greeks for over 2,700 years, we still don't have a good translation of Aristotle, one the main pillars of Western thought. The West is not only pornographic films, sex, violence, and money"—as these were the things that they were mostly criticizing. "These are only the negative aspects of Western culture. It is also Dante, Cervantes, Goethe—if these, too, are the West, then I long to be 'Westoxified.' " I said, "We repeat the criticisms that they themselves make of their own culture and throw it back at them without bothering to understand the essence of Western culture." Given the predominance of the Western culture in our world today, I believe we have no choice but to learn as much as we can about the West and its achievements.

No, I did not take part in the anti-Western crusade of those days, and I never considered it to be something that one could take pride in.

AB: You made the point in passing that the anxiety that you had felt about the new Islamic regime's position vis-à-vis Iranian culture has dissipated, and that you are no longer concerned with such a threat. What was that anxiety based on in the first place?

SM: In the months immediately after the revolution, there was a concerted effort on the part of many within the new regime to denigrate all aspects of the pre-Islamic Iranian history and culture, to cast the history of the Islamic period as nothing more than a history of corrupt [*taghuti*] kings and rulers (except for Karim Khan Zand), to reject all that had been achieved under the Pahlavis by way of modernization, to attack such national symbols as the celebrations of Nowruz and Charshanbeh-Suri as pagan—all in an attempt to "return" history to its only acceptable beginning, i. e., the just rule of Imam Ali in the mid-seventh century. There were attacks even on the Persian language itself.

AB: Whom do you have in mind?

SM: I remember, for example, that after a trip to the Persian Gulf islands and the Arab Emirates, Sadeq Khalkhali had commented in an interview in *Ahvaz* that these were all Islamic territories, and we should not insist on calling them the Persian this or that; we are all Moslems and should not insist that these places necessarily belong to Iran. The Persian Gulf could just as well be called the Islamic Gulf. They started to place a great deal of emphasis on Arabic as the most significant language after Persian, suggesting, among other things, that Arabic should become Iran's diplomatic language. Today, Arabic simply does not have the wide usage and applicability of English or any of the other Western languages. We cannot acquire new scientific and technical knowledge through Arabic. This is not to deny that for understanding our own culture, Arabic is a tremendously important language. But for purposes of comprehending today's world, Arabic is not a particularly effective tool.

In the first year or two after the revolution, they were also directing some of their attacks on Ferdowsi. They changed the name of Ferdowsi University in Mashhad and removed copies of the *Shahnameh* from many bookstore shelves—the latter representing, in all likelihood, an act of self-censorship by the store owners and not a deliberate government policy. At times, they acted as if Ferdowsi were their enemy. But somehow I had the confidence that Ferdowsi would not be defeated and would ultimately impose himself on them. All in all, it appears that the attempts to slight the Iranian national identity by attacking the country's ancient historic traditions and the Persian language failed totally and have now been largely abandoned—or at least moderated considerably. In some ways, this was a repeat of what happened under the Safavids—many examples of which I have given in the book.

AB: Some people think that the symbolic attacks by officials and spokesmen of the postrevolutionary regime to which you are referring were not necessarily anti-"Iranian." Rather, in derogating those symbols that you have described as elements of our national identity, they were attempting to champion their cause of "Islamic universalism" against what they would characterize as "nationalistic sentiments." Otherwise, they, too, must have realized, particularly after the Iraqi invasion of 1980, that Iran's territorial integrity and political survival as a nation are very closely tied to such unifying symbols as the Persian language and our long-standing cultural traditions, be they religious or secular.

SM: If true, this would demonstrate further that the hold of Iranian culture is even stronger than I had thought.

What I must make clear is that I am not necessarily passing a value judgment in favor of the totality of Iranian culture. Certainly, I am not saying that solely because many of its features have survived for centuries, it is good and should therefore be preserved. Indeed, I think that its very continuity—agedness, if you will—poses certain problems and limitations for our society.

AB: Let me turn to a different question. Your emphasis on the role of Persian as the main pillar of Iranian national identity may be interpreted negatively, or indeed offend, the non-Persian-speaking minorities in Iran. I realize that this is not the focus of your work, but I would still like to know your views on this issue.

SM: This is not an area about which I feel qualified to comment. Toward the end of the book, I have pointed out that today the question of Iranian nationality has assumed quite a different meaning. And the whole question of an Iranian national identity—due to such factors as increased mass communications, international contacts, and the positions of outside powers—has become ever more intertwined with what goes on outside of Iran. We can no longer analyze the question of Iranian national identity from the perspective of language and history alone, as I have done in the book. It is something entirely different today.

AB: Does that mean that, in your judgment, the Iranian national identity is based less on the Persian language today than during the historical periods that you discuss in the book?

SM: What I meant to say is that, today, what we have been calling the Iranian national identity—whether it be based on the Persian language, history, religion, or perhaps some combination of the three—is profoundly influenced by what goes on outside of Iran, and therefore, our analysis of it should take full cognizance of that fact. The question of the role of language or languages, too, can only be understood within such a context. The adoption of Turkish, Kurdish, or Baluch as provincial languages, for example, would have significant ramifications, not only for interethnic relations within Iran, but also for Iran's relationship with its neighbors. The whole problem has become intensely politicized, and it is only within a political framework that it can be analyzed meaningfully.

One thing that I am certain of is that promoting the Persian language should certainly not mean suffocating or repressing Turkish or Kurdish—and I am referring to Turkish and Kurdish here because they are the two most widely used languages after Persian in Iran today. If Turkish, for example, is part of the identity of an Azerbaijani, who also considers himself to be an Iranian—as indeed he is—the use of Persian as the official language should in no way threaten or negate his cultural identity. The two aspects of his identity should be allowed to coexist and flourish. But neither would it make sense to adopt a policy under which Turkish, Kurdish, or Baluch effectively becomes the sole language of communication in its respective region of the country. The ideal state of affairs, I believe, is one in which all these languages could exist and thrive alongside each other, each in its area of concentration and in accordance with its own capabilities, but with Persian continuing as the common language of communication among all Iranian ethnic groups.

AB: I take it, then, that you would not favor a "multilingual" language policy for Iran?

SM: I think we would waste a great deal of energy and resources if we were to adopt such a policy. Persian has performed the role of a common, official, or literary language in Iran and elsewhere for well over a thousand years. There is every reason for us to think of it as an essential part of our national identity, both in its historical development and present actuality.

Translator's Preface

Michael Hillmann

In writing *Melliyat va zabân* [Nationality and Language] (1982) in Persian, Shahrokh Meskoob naturally had an Iranian audience in mind. As an expanded revision of the Persian book, this English version also has Iranian readers in mind. But, being in English, the volume naturally addresses non-Iranian, English-speaking readers as well. Consequently dates, bracketed translations of terms and titles, and explanatory footnotes, not in the Persian, appear here. Arabic and Persian book titles and technical terms mostly appear in transliteration and bracketed translations in their first citation. In subsequent citations, the English translation appears, except in the cases of some technical terms for which appropriate English equivalents do not exist. In the case of footnotes, the notation "[MH]" indicates material originating with the translator and not the author. The translation itself attempts to keep the informality of the original, which has meant the sacrifice of literal translation in many places for idiomatic expressions paralleling the Persian.

The transliteration of Arabic and Persian terms into the Latin alphabet follows the Library of Congress system for Arabic (except in a Persian context, in the case of honorifics and titles, etc.) and the system first developed by Nasser Sharify in *Cataloguing of Persian Books* (1959) for Persian, except that the only symbol added to alphabet letters in transliterating Persian is a circumflex to distinguish long /â/ as in "father" or "Tehran" from short /a/ as in "hat" or "Mashhad." Some care has gone into footnote citations of sources so that readers unfamiliar with Persian and Arabic might have access to available translations and non-Persian originals of works that Mr. Meskoob refers to and discusses in the text.

I thank Mage Publishers for inviting me to translate *Melliyat va zabân*. That it is the first book I have translated in twenty-five years in Persian studies implies my sense of the subject's significance to the field and of the timeliness of Mr. Meskoob's book in general intellectual discourse. Readers may assume that ambiguities and infelicities in the English stem from the translation and not the original Persian.

Author's Preface

Shahrokh Meskoob

The essay you have in hand is the rewriting of several lectures given in 1980 and 1981 in Paris, where the Persian edition of this book appeared. This English version exhibits changes and additions to the Persian version, just as that first edition constituted an expanded revision of the original talks. This English text also differs slightly from the original Persian because the English-speaking audience naturally has a different background from the Persian.

The story of the Persian language begins in the ninth century with the establishment of such local Iranian dynasties as the Samanids, the Tâherids and the Saffârids in Greater Khorâsân, Transoxiana and Sistân, in eastern and northeastern Iran. Persian emerged there as a written language, a language of verse and prose. It then achieved formal status and became the second language of the Islamic empire.

This book is a study of the roles played in this process by regional royal courts and their representatives, those who were in the governmental system: on the one hand, administrators and courtiers, and on the other, the Muslim religious scholars or, in today's parlance, the clergy; and likewise the part played by Sufis, or Muslim mystics. In other words, this book deals with the roles of the ruling establishment, of religion, and of Islamic mysticism in the formalization, expansion, achievements, and periods of decline of written Persian.

My focus on the national and cultural role and output of language leads me here to view the subject from a social perspective. Accordingly, I focus primarily on the social base of the three groups cited to discern both the connection each has with nationality and national character, with being Iranian (or, if you will, with "Iranianness") and their relationship with written Persian, with Classical Persian, and the positive or negative roles they have played in it. Consequently the discussion revolves around language and Persian prose as a social phenomenon, and not about literature or thought or other issues relevant to language.

But treatment of the relationship of these groups with language is impossible without discussion of the subject and content of language, especially since I am viewing this relationship primarily from the social base of the groups. For example, if a group or a people by virtue of their social condition and situation utilize a national language, what do they seek to express by so doing? What message do they intend to communicate? Or by contrast, if an Iranian group either ignores the Persian language or rejects it, what does the group communicate by implying that another language better meets its needs? Hence, I naturally devote attention here to the content of the writing of the groups mentioned.

However, with respect to each group, a limited number of particularly telling works or issues receive scrutiny here. Were this book to offer a comprehensive listing or treatment, it would become an epic on reams of paper.

I should add that the choice of these three groups—members of the government establishment, the Muslim clergy, and Sufi mystics—has been a matter of personal predilection. However, although one might choose other classes and discuss their roles in the appearance and spread of Persian as an official language, my choice was not haphazard or lacking in logic insofar as these three have played the principal roles in the matter of language and culture generally. In many instances, of course, it is not possible to segregate these groups as, for example, to distinguish between a Sufi mystic and a religious scholar or among a religious scholar, theologian and court official. In any case, the subject under discussion is the relationship of these three groups with the Persian language from its emergence in the tenth century to the end of the nineteenth century and up to the beginnings of the Constitutional Revolution (1905–1911).

Another issue is that of method. On the basis of the inference I draw from history, or rather, from truth in general (and here "socio-historical truth"), my study is more in the nature of a proposal in the sense of suggestive juxtaposition, of sketching the subject and presenting issues (sometimes only hypotheses) which may stimulate reflection and perhaps shed light on the issues. In the course of the book I hope to communicate to readers my sense of "historical truth." For the moment, suffice it to say that what I am presenting to readers is primarily an invitation to reflect on a corner of Iranian cultural history and to rethink that cultural history, nothing more, and not the exposition of facts which a writer might consider certain and indisputable. My remarks are conceptions about truths, not necessarily truth itself. I will raise contemporary subjects and issues which a cursory look and a preliminary study of Iranian history have brought to mind. I will display these subjects and issues on the field of the reader's vision—selectively, of course. I hope for subsequent discussion of the content, about selection criteria and, naturally, the conclusions. In short, I will be asking as many questions as I will be making statements.

Iranian Nationality
vis-á-vis
Language and History

After the onslaught of the Arabs in the 640s C.E. and the fall of the Sasanian Empire (224–651), we Iranians were in a state of consternation, numbness, and psychological listlessness for at least two centuries. The grand structure of that empire or, in other words, its heavy corpse that had collapsed on the people of Iran, had apparently brought the population to its knees. It was as if the back of a nation had broken beneath the load, especially because the Sasanians' collapse was linked to a military invasion by another people with an alien religion, language and culture, with a military and social power as depicted in the *Târikh-e Sistân* [History of Sistan], *Târikh-e Bokhara* [History of Bokhara], and *Târikhnâmeh-ye Tabari* [Bal'ami's History].[1] The relationship between the Iranian nation and one governmental and cultural order was severed; and Iran fell into another social, governmental and cultural system. Its environment changed. The Sasanian administrative and financial "order" crumbled. When Iran

---

1. [MH] Anonymous, *Târikh-e Sistân* [History of Sistan], edited by Mohammad Taqi Bahâr (Tehran: Ketâbkhâneh-ye Zavvâr, 1960); translated by Milton Gold as *History of Sistân* (Rome: Royal Institute of Translation and Publication and Istituto Italiano per il medio ed estremo oriente, 1976). Abu Nasr b. Ja'far Nasr al-Qobavi (d. 959), *Târikh-e Bokhara* [History of Bokhârâ], edited by M.T. Modarres Razavi (Tehran: Enteshârât-e Bonyâd-e Farhang-e Iran, 1972). Abu 'Ali Mohammad b. Mohammad (fl. 946–973), *Târikhnâmeh-ye Tabari*, 3 volumes (Tehran, 1987), hereafter referred to as Bal'ami's History.

emerged from beneath the rubble, it suddenly saw itself in an unfamiliar, alien land, finally managing after much hardship and risk to free itself.

It took two hundred years of consternation at this homelessness and alienation before Iran was able gradually to revive and resume its life. I am talking about Iranians as a single nation, as a people with an identity of their own, and not as scattered individuals. From the end of the seventh century, a great many individual Iranians sought to participate in the expansion of Islam and Arabic language and culture, and became representatives of these phenomena. Be that as it may, I repeat that in order to survive and in pursuing their life as a single people Iranians took different paths, several of which I mention here.

For example, the landowners and local property owners [*dehqâns*] who had formerly assisted the government in administering villages, collecting taxes, conscripting soldiers and the like, adjusted in this period to the governmental system of the new Muslim Arab rulers, and became the financial and administrative agents of the government and its agents outside of the large cities. They were the government's link with the peasantry. In this situation and social role, they were able to preserve some economic and cultural privileges. Their historical past, and the mere fact of their continued existence as a broad class, caused them to become to some extent the preservers and transmitters of Iranian language and culture. Their attachment to Iran was such that during the tenth and eleventh centuries the word *dehqân* denoted "Iranian." Iranian readers will recall these lines by the epic poet Ferdowsi (d.c. 1020):

> From Iranians and from Turks and from Arabs
> A race will appear in our midst,
> Neither dehqân [Iranian] nor Turk nor Arab,
> Whose words will be frivolous.[2]

Another example is a *qasideh* by Abu Hanifeh Eskâfi with the following couplet in which *dehqân* appears with the denotation "Iranian" in contrast with "Arab": "Ma'mun, the likes of whom has never been seen since among Muslim kings, neither by Arabs nor Persians [*dehqân*]."

---

2. [MH] Abolqâsem Ferdowsi, *Shâhnâmeh* [Book of Kings]. The handiest English translation is Reuben Levy's abridged prose version called *The Epic of the Kings* (Chicago, IL: University of Chicago Press, 1967).

In contrast, some leading Iranian families after converting to Islam chose the road of the caliphal court, where they achieved high stations. If they were grounded in Iranian culture, especially in customs and ceremonies, they endeavored to put them into practice at the caliphal court with the result that Sasanian monarchical traditions in royal ceremonies, their splendor and wasteful extravagance, and many of the ways of governmental administrators and courtly behavior became a model for the 'Abbâsid caliphal court (750–1258), especially after the construction of a new capital at Baghdad (in 762) near the old Sasanian capital at Ctesiphon.

Along with their service to the caliphate, some of these Iranians also had an eye out for the land of their fathers. I am thinking of the Barmaki family, the Sahmids, the Nowbakhtis, the Tâherids in all likelihood, and other such families. The interest of some of them in Shiism, their respect for the family of the Prophet Mohammad (and a consequent lack of respect for the 'Abbâsids) are mute signs of this sort. The question as to whether the hearts of some of these families were not with the caliphate but were elsewhere is not here at issue. But their ambivalent situation—their being Iranian and presenting themselves as Arabs—did not allow them to pass unscathed through the perilous positions of emirate and vizierate. We know what a sad end most of them came to.

The transfer of written culture, the translation of surviving Pahlavi books and works into Arabic, was another means utilized by some for preserving that which had remained from the past. The newly converted Muslim, Ibn al-Moqaffa' (c.720–c.757) and his works, are one example, and the most outstanding. In order to avoid any later misperceptions, allow me to digress by saying that I do not imply by any means that a group of scholars who loved Iran, out of a sense of patriotism and without any other expectation, risked every sort of danger to come forward and consciously set about translating Pahlavi works into Arabic and other languages in order to preserve Iranian culture. No, to pursue a particular cause in investigating historical currents and events is misleading, for the simple reason that the causes of events at origin are various, numerous and very often even conflicting; the different causes sometimes seem to negate one another. Here also one has to bear in mind different motives, ranging from worldly and personal motives—service to new rulers, attaining high position and wealth and making a living—to love of culture and love of truth; the cultural environment at the beginning of Islamic civilization; thirst for knowledge and information; and the need for an old yet defeated people to survive. In any case, we should not see only one aspect of reality (which usually exhibits various faces).

Alongside these prominent Iranians, some scholars, with or even without an interest in group or national feeling, were inclined to seek a reconciliation or compatibility between Koranic and Iranian myths and legends: a reconciliation, as it were, between religion and custom. In this fashion, Iranian myths found a legitimacy in the Islamic environment. The faithful accepted them, and they survived. In addition, because Islam considered Zoroastrians as people possessing a legitimate holy book, this synthesis and reconciliation were feasible. As a result, for example, they had come to think of Zoroaster and Abraham or Jamshid and Solomon as one and the same. Two meaningful illustrations are the *Târikh al-rusul wa'l-mulûk* [History of the Prophets and the Kings] by Tabari (d. 932)[3] and *Mojmal al-tavârîkh va'l-qesas* [Summary of Histories and Stories] (1126, of unknown authorship). These two histories, which Iranians wrote in Arabic and Persian respectively, both exhibit this harmony and reconciliation of mythologies.

Of particular note, as examples of Iranian cultural resistance for the purpose of survival, are various deep-rooted and long-term religious, spiritual and social movements. I shall turn later to Shiism and Sufism, the Sho'ubiyeh movement, and Isma'ilism.

Besides such indirect resistance or direct intellectual, religious and cultural resistance, Iranians here and there sporadically fought with the Arabs in order to survive, and revolted against them. Examples include Beh'âfarid (d.c. 749), al-Moqanna' (d. 778), and Bâbak (d.c. 838), leaders of insurrections in northeastern and northwestern Iran, and sometimes wars of ten and twenty years' duration.[4]

During the period in which we Iranians emerged from defeat and consternation to the time when we could again stand on our own feet,

---

3. Mohammad Ibn Jarîr al-Tabari, *Târikh al-rusul wa'l-mulûk* [History of the Prophets and the Kings], hereafter referred to as Tabari's History. Numerous portions of Tabari's History are available in English translations, the most relevant among them: *The Ancient Kingdoms* (Albany, NY: SUNY Press, 1987).

4. [MH] Elton Daniel, *The Political and Social History of Khorâsân under Abbasid Rule, 747–820* (Minneapolis, MN: Bibliotheca Islamica, 1979), reviews existing data on these insurrections and draws current scholarly conclusions about their nature.

we persevered as a people in two ways, indirectly and directly or, in other words, culturally and militarily. And after four hundred years we achieved two results: defeat and victory. We suffered defeat in direct confrontation, in direct opposition and contest for political and social aims, for separatism from the Arab victors, from the Baghdad caliphate, and from the religion of Islam. But we achieved victory in the preservation of nationality and language. We maintained one nationality or, perhaps better put, our national identity, our Iranianness, through the blessing of language, by means of the vitality of Persian as a refuge. Despite political fragmentation into numerous geographical units and with Arab, Iranian and Turkic governments, Iran (in particular, Khorâsân) was not dissimilar in those days from ancient Greece, or Germany and Italy until the second half of the nineteenth century. In all of these countries, one people and one national group with a common language existed with a degree of common culture alongside differences in government. They possessed cultural unity without political unity, unity in roots but fragmentation in branches and leaves.

History as Self-Definition

One characteristic of history is that it gives meaning to itself. In this regard, it resembles association of ideas in the mind, in the memory: thinking of a friend leads one to think of another friend and from friendship to the remembrance of love and from youthful love to youth to the remembrance of a thousand other twists and turns, like a chain, the chain-like tresses of the beloved. The business of history is obviously not that simple, but it is similar. Every great historical event—by great I mean an important, influential action, regardless of its moral character—every great historical event leads to a return to history itself, like a folding mirror that reflects its own image upon itself, albeit slightly distorted. An event that takes place in a particular time and that turns a people upside down brings new problems that everyone must come to grips with, overcome and control, or come to terms with, surrender and give in. Something that occurs in the present time of a nation becomes in any case a reason for them to think about the causal context of that event, which is to say its history, in order to comprehend within their own limits their present time and path and find a solution in their future, which is beyond human control. This inevitable contemplation about the past gives history a new meaning, because we are looking at it from a new angle in search of effects of the historical event on us. And we achieve a new understanding from it.

For example, the effect of the French Revolution on life in Europe and thereafter in the history of the world is obvious: the effects of revolution after revolution. But this revolution changed the understanding of history, the social forces having a hand in history, the relations of these forces and their effects on social evolution (i.e., history). Not only did it change the meaning of history, it also brought many of these issues onto the carpet.

The fact that history is social change, that it is irreversible, that it does not have a monolithic and continual motion but rather has ups and downs and unbalanced movement, the fact that forces other than those which are patently obvious figure in the evolution of history and its structure and that the historian seeking truth must discover those, the authenticity of events, and the givens in history and following that historical positivism . . . most of these issues came to the fore after the French Revolution and under its influence. And if some of them existed prior to the Revolution, they were now scrutinized more deeply and from various new angles. I should add that Hegel and his historicist philosophy is a product of the French Revolution. Phenomenology of the Spirit, perhaps the most significant fundamental and schematic effect of his thought, is the exposition of the development and evolution of the Spirit in human history. In Hegel even the absolute, that is the absolute Spirit, is also susceptible to history and finds its own fulfillment in history.

An Iranian example would be the Constitutional Movement (1905–1911), a national revolution which sought justice and freedom. The framing of the issue of nationality both then and afterwards generated new interest in pre-Islamic history, especially since with the accessing of scattered data from European sources that period was thought of as Iran's golden age. A little before the Constitutional Revolution, accompanying the appearance of national feeling and awareness, there occurred a sense of disgust at traditional historiography together with a rejection of the old understanding of history and a new interest in its social meaning and role. In a brief period, numerous histories unprecedented in style and conception were written or translated.

On the subject of *Â'ineh-ye Sekandar* [Alexander's Mirror] by Mirza Aqa Khan Kermâni (1853–1897), the prominent historian Fereydun Âdamiyat (b. 1920) writes: "He wrote the first volume of the history of Iran, from the beginning to the decline of the Sasanians and the rise of Islam. This was the first modern, scholarly history of ancient Iran by an Iranian historian based on his own study and the research of European scholars." Mirza Aqa Khan Kermâni himself wrote to Malkom Khan (1833–1910): "Such a history is necessary both to fell the tree of oppression and to bring to life the power of nationality in the disposition of the people of Iran."[5]

For Mirza Aqa Khan Kermâni, history had two chief roles and aims. One was the overthrow of oppressive despotism; the other was the strengthening of national sentiment, and that in a period in which Iranians were subject to the colonialist onslaught of other governments, particularly Russia and Great Britain. In essence, for him the aim of history was identical with the aim of the Constitutional Revolution.

Not only with respect to history was there a revival of interest, but also with respect to language, one of the principal later fruits being 'Ali Akbar Dehkhodâ's encyclopedic dictionary called *Loghatnâmeh* [Word Book] (1953–1966). Such people as Hasan Pirniyâ (1871–1935), Dehkhodâ (1879–1956), the historian Hasan Taqizâdeh (1873–1970) and the scholar Ebrâhim Purdâvud (1886–1968) were the products of the Constitutional Revolution; they were among the young people of that period, although their work was completed in the following period. I mention these four merely as examples. Other distinguished scholars, such as Mohammad Taqi Bahâr (1886–1951), Mohammad Qazvini (1877–1949), 'Abbâs Eqbâl (1896–1955) and Ahmad Kasravi (1890–1946), are important in their own right.

Let me summarize and move along. It will be strange if the Islamic Revolution of 1978–79 does not likewise stimulate Iranians to return to their own history and reexamine the past from the vantage point and behind the windowpanes of the present. This is bound to happen.

Return to the Past

From these introductory comments, I would like to draw the following conclusion: after suffering defeat at the hands of the Arabs and after converting to Islam, the Iranian people also returned to the past. They turned back from one great historical event to history. Like Arabs,

---

5. Fereydun Âdamiyat, *Andisheh'hâ-ye Mirza Aqa Khan Kermâni* [The Ideas of Mirza Aqa Khan Kermâni] (Tehran: Enteshârât-e Payâm, 1978), p. 55.

Iranians were now Muslims, but they had a different language. In the tenth century, when they organized their own first regional governments and concomitantly wrote and composed poetry in their own language, they assumed the character of a discrete and independent people or nation. They were well aware of this fact. After four hundred years, when all other means and attempts to secede from Arab domination had failed, Iranians turned to history, some with the aim of secession from Islam as well. For their own preservation as a separate nation, they returned to their own history, and took a stand in the stronghold of their language. They turned to the two things that differentiated them from other Muslims.

Within a period of approximately fifty years, from the latter part of the ninth century, there arose an interest in the heroic, epic narratives called *shâhnâmeh* [book of the kings] and in compiling these.[6] Of course, because interest in *shâhnâmeh*s had existed before this, it would be more accurate to say that interest in compiling *shâhnâmeh*s (which were Iranian mythology and history) suddenly became general and ubiquitous. We know about the *Khwadây-nâmag* [Book of the Lords/ Kings] compiled toward the end of the Sasanian period, which was the original source for the *shâhnâmeh* par excellence, that of Ferdowsi.

On the other hand, we know that epic and history were once thought to be interconnected and to be one and the same. Ferdowsi's *Shâhnâmeh* (c. 1010) is the premier example. In any case, in this short period, we have records of the *shâhnâmeh* of Abu al-Mo'ayyad Balkhi, the *shâhnâmeh* of Abu 'Ali Mohammad b. Ahmad Balkhi, the *shâhnâmeh* of Abu Mansur 'Abdorrazzâq and the *shâhnâmeh* of Daqiqi (d.c. 980), then the *Shâhnâmeh* (c. 1010) of Ferdowsi, the *Garshâspnâmeh* [Book of Garshâsp] of Asadi Tusi (fl. 1060s), and the *Borzunâmeh*. *Shâhnâmeh* fever, the fever of epic and history, the return to origins and the past, a grasping for the roots of nationality, enveloped everyone; all these works were composed in Khorâsân, and all in Persian.[7]

---

6. On the meaning of the term *shâhnâmeh* [book of the kings], see Jalâl Matini, "Dar ma'ni-ye shâhnâmeh," *Irânshenâsi* 2 (1991): 742–754; English summary, English section, pp. 113-114.

7. [MH] E.g. Asadi Tusi, *Garshâspnâmeh* [Book of Garshâsp], edited by Habib Yaghmâ'i (Tehran: Tahuri, 1975, 2nd printing); translated by Henri Massé as *Le livre de Gershâsp* (Paris: P. Geuthner, 1926–1951). Abu Mansur Mohammad b. Ahmad Daqiqi, *Divân-e Abu Mansur Ebn-e Ahmad Daqiqi Tusi* [Collection Poems of Daqiqi], edited by Javâd Shari'at (Tehran, Enteshârât-e Asâtir, 1989).

A short time before, Zoroastrian priests had likewise gathered and recorded their own scriptures in the Pahlavi language, among them *Dênkard, Bundahishn, Bahman Yasht, Yâdgâr-e Jâmâsp*, to preserve them from being scattered and damaged.[8] For them, these works did not deal with a dead past, but with a living religion in which they believed and were involved on a daily basis for the sake of this world and the next. If these works, scattered and disorganized, passed from hand to hand among the priests for approximately two hundred years, without being compiled and put into proper order, perforce one of the reasons was the disturbed and agitated state of the Zoroastrian faithful themselves, and the disintegration of the religious establishment and the priests in charge of the preservation of such things. In any case, whatever we may conjecture, the historical reality is that in basically a single period, in the same period in which Muslim Iranians turned to epic, history and the past, non-Muslim Iranians likewise were engaged in compiling their own legacy, pulling themselves together and at least giving some order to the chaos of their religious books.

At the beginning of the tenth century Iranian dynastic families achieved monarchical power and semi-independence from the Baghdad caliphate. Such were the Samanids, the Saffârids, the Tâherids and the Farighunids. What is remarkable is that all of them also endeavored to trace themselves back to pre-Islamic Iran. They produced bogus lineages and family trees. The Samanids linked themselves to the legendary revolutionary Bahrâm Chubin and from him to Manuchehr, the mythological Pishdâdi monarch, i.e., to the beginning of "history" and the first appearance of the Iranians. The lineage of Ahmad b. Sahl, a leading Samanid prince, was traced back to Yazdagerd III, the last Sasanian monarch (d. 751), and that of Abu Mansur ibn 'Abdorrazzâq (d. 961), the governor of Khorâsân and the compiler of a *shâhnâmeh*, to the mythological warrior Giv, son of Gudarz. Even the Saffârids, born of coppersmiths, were linked to Anushirvân (ruled 531–579) and the Tâherids to Rostam. The Buyids, the sons of the fisherman Buyeh, claimed descent from the Sasanian monarch Bahram Gur (ruled 420–438). In this fashion, Muslim kings registered in their own lineage non-Muslim, Iranian dynasties and kings of the past in order to appropriate for themselves the exclusive right to a historical link with those kings.

---

8. Aturpât-i Emêtân (9th century), *The Wisdom of the Sasanian Sages (Dênkard VI)*, translated by Shaul Shaked (Boulder, CO: Westview Press, 1979).

None of this is unusual. What is strange is that forging links with
the past became so common and such a sign of governmental legitimacy that former Turkish slaves and now invaders, the Ghaznavids
(ruled 998–1040) and the Saljuqs, foreign newcomers, also traced their
lineage to the Sasanian Yazdagerd and the mythological Turânian ruler
Afrâsiyâb. Through this maneuver they became people of noble birth
and lineage. Then, once in possession of a viceregency from Baghdad,
their government achieved legitimacy.

All of what has been said shows that a sort of national feeling, the
feeling of being Iranian (and as a consequence the feeling of not being
Arab), was widespread, at least in the east, the northeast, the north and
the northwest of Iran. Something that for some time had existed in the
form of a spiritual ethnicity, a universal but personal sense, part of the
social psychology, reached a culmination in the tenth century with the
formation of the semi-independent or independent Iranian dynasties
already mentioned. These dynasties, which were the product of
national feeling, served from the very beginning as guardians and
transmitters of national identity in the realm of language. The story
of the Saffârid leader Ya'qub Lays and Mohammad-e Vasif Sagzi is
famous. As the *History of Sistan* records it, after Ya'qub obtained the
governorship of Herât, Pushang, Sistan, Kâbol, Kermân and Fârs from
Mohammad b. Tâher "the poets composed poems for him in Arabic .
. . then Ya'qub said: 'Why must they say something I do not understand?' Then Mohammad-e Vasif composed a poem in Persian, which
was the first poem composed by a Persian." This was perhaps about
870 C.E. Iranians know well the opening couplet of this first Persian
poem, which goes: 'O Prince toward whom the princes of the world
high and low / Are slaves, servants, and captives.' Similarly, the
Samanid prince Nasr b. Ahmad ordered *Kalileh and Demneh* be translated into Persian. In the words of Ferdowsi: "It was in Arabic until
the time of Nasr. / When he became king of victory [*nasr*] in the world
/ He commanded that they write it in Persian [*pârsi-ye dari*], / And that
settled the matter."

Another Samanid monarch, Amir Nuh b. Mansur, requested that
Daqiqi (d.c. 980) produce a verse *Shâhnâmeh* (Abu Mansuri's *Shâhnâmeh* had been in prose). And Abu al-Mo'ayyad Balkhi wrote *'Ajâyeb-e
barr va bahr yâ 'ajâyeb-e boldân* [Wonders of Land and Sea or the
Marvels of Different Cities] "for the king of the world, the prince of

Khorâsân, by order of Nuh b. Mansur, the Prince of the Faithful."[9] A final example is the case of another Samanid king, Abu Sâleh Mansur b. Nuh, at whose behest and foresight Persian translations of the Koran, Tabari's Commentary, and Tabari's History were undertaken.

In any case, after various efforts and finally after four hundred years, Iranians became a nation with a separate identity special to themselves by means of a return to the past, to their own history and with the establishment of Iranian governments and reliance on the Persian language. A new people with a new religion and civilization had emerged with awareness of their own identity. The past was the refuge for this identity and language its stage. Iran was a new tree, nurtured in the climate of Islam, but growing in the soil of its own national memory.

Before Islam and After Islam

Of course in earlier periods as well, we Iranians were a nation with an identity special to ourselves. We possessed a vision of Iran and things Iranian, and we thought it important to be Iranian. We called others *anirân* or non-Iranian. The world was divided into two groups: Iranian and non-Iranian. These Iranians—I am focusing primarily on the Sasanian period (224–651)—had a sort of common world view and a generally common mythology. These myths were the foundation of their religion and view of existence, of God and human beings and the world. It would be better to say that they had a sort of "relationship" in myths which led to an ideological and intellectual kinship. Besides this, their system of government was a unit with a "king of kings" at its head.

The network of this system pervaded the empire, and subjects who were Iranian had a sort of connection with it. There was also an economic and social structure of transactions in which everyone was involved and shared, and people lived on the basis of the role they played in it. For that matter, all of them from king to beggar had a place in "Aêriyana-vaêjah" (in the land of "Khaonîrath," the central one of the seven countries of the world). Theirs was a mythological geography, that is, an image of a location beyond other places which

---

9. Zabihollâh Safâ, *Ganjineh-ye sokhan* [Treasury of Speech], vol. I (Tehran: Tehran University Press, 1969) pp. 166–68.

they did not consider an ordinary geographical location or a land like other lands.

These important and meaningful factors presumably became the matrix distinguishing us Iranians from others—good or bad is beside the point. Now, whether or not these factors had been correctly chosen, this much is certain, that the distinction existed. Iranians had an identity peculiar to themselves of which they were aware, perhaps like the Greeks who divided people into Greek and "barbarian" (meaning foreign, strange). But during the Islamic period, our identity lost these factors and this matrix and consequently found another character and personality. The factors cited, considered separately, constituted the essence of difference between Iranians and non-Iranians, while the bulk of the elements constituting our identity during the tenth century were stimuli for unification and mingling of Iranian and non-Iranian. In such fashion we emerged once again as a young nation or people.

The reason was that in the Islamic period our Iranian religion was the same as that of the Arabs and other Muslims, like all Muslims, in which regard we were all similar. Instead of the Sasanian government, there was the Baghdad caliphate, and a caliph at its head. If the Sasanian government was peculiarly Iranian, the Baghdad caliphate was special for Muslims. Likewise, the economic and social structure of the Islamic empire in its general aspects was the same everywhere and for all peoples. These were all homogenizing elements which reduced the separateness of one people or nation from others and caused them to intermingle and become one. Only with respect to two things were we Iranians separate from other Muslims: history and language, the two factors on which we proceeded to build our own identity as a people or nation. History was our currency, the provisions for the way, and our refuge. Language was the foundation, floor, and refuge for the soul, a stronghold within which we stood.

It would be a shame to conclude this part of the discussion without citing Ferdowsi (940–1020) again. At most it can be said that Ferdowsi was the vivifier of our Iranian nationality. This statement is not very precise. Before Ferdowsi our national feelings had come to life. At the beginning of the tenth century we were a newly arrived, vital and young nation. For example, when Rudaki (d. 940) produced that poem of his which begins, "Live happy with black-eyed ones, happy / for the world is but a fantasy and empty air," he was giving vent to the *cri de coeur* of just such a nation.[10] The nation had entered the arena and was all for life, without excessive gullibility or misgivings. Even Rudaki's complaint at old age, in the *qasideh* about teeth in which he says, "Whatever teeth there were have been ground down and fallen out," is not a complaint arising out of helplessness and hopelessness. But I digress. I wanted to say something about Ferdowsi, whose propitious existence led to the re-creation of two essential elements of our nationality in a great work where the two coalesced into a single body. His *Shâhnâmeh* is the heroic, epic history and language of a people who are alive in their history and language. It is the ideal of Iranian nationality, and later becomes the most important cultural factor in preserving Iranian nationality. As Ferdowsi himself says:

> This marvelous book of kings of yore
> I composed in my own masterful style.
> I created a world of speech like heaven;
> No one has better sown the seed of speech.
> I toiled a great deal in these thirty years;
> With this Persian I brought to life *'ajam*
> [Iran/Persia, Iranians/Persians].

Language and National Feeling

As for the already discussed role of language in the formation of Iranian nationality, language has performed such a function among other peoples as well. Language is both the most essential and the most common means of communication in daily human life and the most appropriate means for bringing into existence and giving shape to ideas, and likewise for describing and explaining feelings. One might call language the substance of thought, just as stone or clay is the matter of sculpture. Thought finds corporeality in language. In order for a scattered people to accept form, to possess a shape or substance, become aware of one another's thoughts and find mutuality of feeling and as a result become an organic collective, a nation, they have no better means than language. Language is the best, but not the only, means for giving shape to a nation or people. Arts and other social and cultural factors usually accompany it. Dancing and music in India, painting in China, architecture and sculpture and again music and painting in Europe illustrate the role of factors other than language in

---

10.   Rudaki, *Gozideh-ye ash'âr* [Selected Poems], compiled and edited by Ja'far She'ar and Hasan Anvari (Tehran: Amir Kabir, 1986), p. 122.

the genesis of a nation and its character. At the same time, we know that great art has a twofold character: it is at one and the same time both universal and general, and national and regional (as opposed to science, which is only universal and general).

However, we Iranians were without almost all of these factors (except for architecture) in creating our national identity. In Islam the arts I have mentioned are not permissible. Thus our task was more difficult: our nationality had no abode except language. Before concluding this part of the discussion, allow me to make one more point.

The spread of Christianity was essentially not based on military force; that is to say, in the process of its expansion in general, different peoples did not confront one another militarily and politically. For this reason, the official and written languages of the new European nations (Christian nations) were not obliged to confront religion in the course of their appearance and creation. The Latin language was the language of religion and culture. The role of the Arabic language in the Islamic empire is often compared to that of the Latin language in medieval Europe. This comparison is only valid up to a point, because the relation between the Latin language and Christianity is otherwise different from the link between the Arabic language and Islam.

Arabic was the language of a people who took a new religion with energetic force to other lands. Their scripture (the word of God) was likewise in the same language. Thus, any sort of national or cultural independence, any sort of emergence from the material and spiritual control of the dominant people necessarily raised the issue of the Arabic language, vis-à-vis which we Iranians had to assume some position. We defined our own cause with respect to it. The language of religion and the language of Arabic government had, unfortunately, become one, and using a language, Arabic or Persian, had acquired a political and "national" significance.

Abu Hanifa (699–767), a leader of one of the four chief Sunni sects, was a prominent religious scholar. But even he faced serious criticism when he suggested that the Persian language was as legitimate for prayer as the Arabic language: ". . . one of these disagreements is very important in terms of religious politics. The official language of worship in Islam is Arabic. All of the tasks of worship are carried out with the language of the Koran. Now if a person is unable to speak Arabic, is he able to recite the *fâtiha* and such prayers in his mother tongue? And Abu Hanifa, who was of the Iranian race, was the one person who counted this permissible. His reason was that 'This Koran had also been revealed in earlier books . . . which were presumably in a language other than Arabic. Therefore non-Arabs have the right to consider them Korans.' Abu Hanifa's enemies accused him of Zoroastrian inclinations because he had made this unprecedented statement about the Persian language."[11]

To spread and popularize Arabic, counterfeit Prophetic Traditions were even created. A Tradition of Abu Horayra has it that God is fed up with Persian speech, the language of devils of Khuzistan and hell-dwellers of Bokhara, and that the language of heaven is Arabic. In contrast, another Prophetic Tradition (presumably from an Iranian) claimed that Persian and Arabic are both languages of residents of heaven.[12]

The original languages of the Gospels were Greek and Hebrew. Later appeared the translation of holy writ into Latin, as the language of the Church, the language of the religion of the Christians. The language of the Koran had a link with the people bearing the religion, whereas the language of the Gospels had no link with any people or nation (as the bearer of religion). The former was the language of the Arab people and had an influential political and historical role to the advantage of the government of the Arabs. The latter was completely without effect in terms of establishing the government of a people. Of course, the Latin language was a means at the disposal of the church hierarchy; but the Church was not a nation or a people or anything of that sort; it resembled a government more than a nation. Furthermore, from the period of the domination of Europe by the Roman Empire, that is, before the appearance of Christianity, the

---

11. Ignac Goldziher, *Dars'há'i darbáreh-ye eslám* [Vorlesugen über den Islam, 1925], translated by 'Alinaqi Monzavi (Tehran: Enteshárát-e Kamángir, 1978), p. 101. [MH] Idem, *Introduction to Islamic Theology and Law* (Princeton, NJ: Princeton University Press, 1981).

12. Zabihollâh Safa, *Târikh-e adabiyât dar Iran*, 5 volumes (Tehran: Entesharât-e Ebn-e Sinâ/Entesharât-e Ferdowsi, 195?–1984) 1: 146. [MH] On the history of Persian literature, the two most-used English-language sources are: Edward G. Browne, *A Literary History of Persia*, 4 vols. (Cambridge: Cambridge University Press, 1969, first printed 1902–1924); and Jan Rypka, *History of Iranian Literature*, edited by Karl Jahn (Dordrecht, Holland: Reidel, 1968). *Persian Literature*, edited by Ehsan Yarshater (Albany, NY: SUNY Press, 1988), features a thematic approach, but does not treat pre-modern Persian prose writing.

Latin language had been the cultural language of Europeans. Through this language a sort of cultural unity had been established in parts of Europe. That is why it would be erroneous to compare the roles of Arabic and Latin in the two cultures of Islam and Christianity, without marking their differences.

In any case, in the West as well, language was the most essential and distinguishing feature of one people against another. But insofar as the Europeans had accepted Christianity centuries earlier, when each people or nation became aware of its own identity, language, because it was the showcase for this self-awareness, turned to expressing the history of its own people or nation, without any resulting incompatibility with religion or the language of religion. Let me cite a few more names as examples: Wolfram von Eschenbach's *Perzeval* (c. 1205) and the *Nibelungenlied* (17th c.) of the Germans, *Chansons de gestes* (12th c.) of the French, and *Beowulf* (10th c.), *Poema del mio Cid* (12th c.) and Ariosto's *Orlando Furioso* (1532), of the English, Spaniards, and Italians respectively. These examples at the same time bring to mind the *Iliad* and the *Odyssey* and the cultural role enjoyed by epics in the formation of peoples and nations. In any case, the nations of the West at the beginning of their activity returned to their own "history" and "historical culture." Interestingly, however, when they recited the material and shared religious (Christian) stories in their national language, they created them as their own national works. The melding of Christianity, which was the religion throughout Europe, and chivalry, which was both a European phenomenon and had a local (i.e., national) character, facilitated the "nationalizing" of Christian heroes, such as the Christian Perceval, who as a knight traveled in search of the Holy Grail. In the Middle Ages, Parsifal/Perceval was both a German hero and a French hero, a status not possible for Roland or Siegfried to achieve. For although the epic actions of Roland were also religious and he fought against infidels, they were infidels who attacked France and no other place. His struggle thus assumed a national character, within the limits of the French nation and not beyond it.

But in Western European countries as well, national languages intruded upon religion. In the course of the Protestant Reformation in opposition to the Papal court and the Roman Catholic faith, German became a language of the Church for the first time, and Martin Luther translated the Bible into this language in the sixteenth century. A little later the same thing happened in England. The book that had been extant only in Latin, the language of Christian religion, now appeared in all languages.

On the Subject of Iranian Identity

As described earlier, in the tenth century we Iranians, a people who had undergone the test of defeat, shouldered the knapsack of our history and stood on the territory of our language. An ancient people sprang up anew, like all other Muslims yet different from the rest on account of a distinctive identity and awareness of this distinction, on account of an Iranian awareness of being Iranian. The tree of Iranianness grew on the earth of the Persian language and in the climate of Islam.

In essence, identity is a reactive matter. Attention to self becomes meaningful in relation to others and from being with them. Being oneself means not being another. It means having differences from others, and preserving separateness and distance even while enjoying links or even intermingling. This perception is proper to human beings as social animals. Since it accrues meaning through and from others, whenever a people face danger and onslaught from these others, they are naturally stimulated to greater attention to their own identity. The situation resembles that of a body which prepares itself for defense when an illness invades it. When it is not ill, the body has no need for its defense system. Of course, contact with others is different from the harm that illness causes the body, but the analogy makes my point clear.

Moreover, awareness of identity is a passive matter. Yet concern about having an identity is a negative thing in the sense that it is a reaction, usually not voluntary or spontaneous. These words have not been employed as synonyms. The state of knowing (or awareness) and the state of self-stimulation have three meanings and three separate personal states. In any case, the negative force is imposed upon a person from outside. When it somehow places all or part of a person in a threatened position, this concern surfaces. In human society also, nations facing danger perforce become concerned about their own identity. On the other hand, if powerful or victorious nations take note of their identity, it is not out of worry and anxiety, but for other reasons. It is in order to preserve, or even to increase, military-political and economic or cultural superiority. It is not passive, but rather active, and for the most part belligerent and aggressive.

In recent Iranian history, that is, from late August 1953 onward (the fall of Mosaddeq and the restoration of the Shah), as the influence of America in Iran became greater and as American culture and aspects of American ways of life found their way into our midst, an issue raised by Iranian intellectuals ever since the beginning of the Constitutional Revolution—by people with such differing views as Mirza Malkom Khan (1833–1910), Shaykh Fazlollâh Nuri, Taqizâdeh and Kasravi—grew every day more urgent: how to account for oneself vis-à-vis the West, and how to behave toward the West. The political, economic, and cultural onslaught of the West on us came to be seen as "Weststruckness," being blighted by the West, in the words of the social critic Jalal Al-e Ahmad (1923–1969), on the analogy of aphids destroying wheat.[13]

I use the recent period as an illustration; otherwise discussion of this issue is irrelevant. Let me merely take the opportunity to recall that the discourse which took place during recent decades in the context of "Weststruckness" by Al-e Ahmad and others on this complicated and multifaceted subject was superficial and hasty, and arose from political biases and from behind ideological glasses which necessarily had preconceived results. For this reason I called it "negative." Of course, one must admit that political conditions during the later Pahlavi era (1953–1978), the existence of censorship and so on, were not without effect in keeping political thinking and discussions of this sort superficial. Today, too, the same situation obtains. With the prevailing bias, narrow-mindedness, and enmity, how much open discussion can take place, in what forum and in what form?

Let me end this brief digression and return to the Iranian past. The arrival of Islam in Iran, in contrast to the spread of Christianity in Europe, was linked with political and military invasion. Iran suffered religious, political, and military subjugation. For this reason, after they came to their senses again, Iranians either had to accept the language and nationality of their conquerors as they had accepted their religion, or accept only Islam and in other respects remain a people with their own identity.

We should remember that Islam was a world religion unconcerned with nations, tribes, and race: *innamâ al-mu'minin ikhwah* [believers

---

13. [MH] Jalal Al-e Ahmad, *Gharbzadegi* [Weststruckness] (Tehran, 1962, 1964), and much translated, e.g., by John Green and Ahmad 'Alizâdeh (Costa Mesa, CA: Mazda Publishers, 1982).

are brothers]. But not only were its proselytizers and promoters from particular people and tribes, not only had they not forgotten this characteristic, and not only did they take pride in this and boast accordingly to others; but also, among themselves as well, they continually exhibited prejudice in matters of tribal superiority, race and lineage, and fought over these. This contradiction between Islam and a particular group of Muslims (the Arabs) existed from the outset and would appear to remain intact today. For even in the 1980s, the army of Iraq attacked Iran in the name of the "army of Qâdesiyeh," as much as to say: "Don't forget that we Arabs are those very people who long ago taught you a lesson; we are different from you."

In any case, Iranians became Muslim, but remained Iranian. They joined Islam while maintaining their own identity, which was no easy task, because in the matter of identity religion (Islam) was more important than land (Iran). Wherein lay the sources and essence of human identity in those days? By what means did a human being then come to grips with his circumstances and with what criteria did he assess himself, with what touchstone did he assay himself? We know that in the past the customary view people had of the world was religious, i.e., God is ancient, omniscient, omnipotent, and eternal. Such an eternal God created the world and the hereafter. In this view, that which has genuineness is not the relation between a human being and the insentient and transitory world of creation; that which forms the inner kernel of his identity is the nature of his link with heaven, not with earth. Being Jewish, Christian or Muslim is more important than being Iranian, Spanish or whatever. "The homeland is not Egypt, Iraq, and Syria." A homeland in the sense of the abode of a true life and a spiritual existence is not this or that land, because the earth itself likewise becomes possessed of truth and quality only in its relation with heaven. Only with the Renaissance and after, and in Europe, does the earth take the place of heaven; nature attains greater value than what lies beyond it, and the relation between human beings and the earth on which they live changes.

A little earlier I stated that identity and concern with and awareness of self have meaning in relation to concern with the existence of others. Now I say that the origin and essence of human identity lies in the nature of their links with the world above, with God. Perhaps here a difficulty or a contradiction might seem to arise, but in fact there is no contradiction. Rather, the issue of identity has been viewed in two different arenas, the sociological and the existential. The first is the relation of a person with others, in society. The second is the relation of a person with existence, in the world. This look at the issue is not twofold in interpretation; rather it is a focus on one subject in two arenas, on two strata and in two dimensions.

In the period under discussion, the business of identity in both positions confronted Iranians head on or, rather, was forced upon them. In the ontological dimension, in the knowledge and inquiry of oneself from the world above, an identity had found a new character, it had appeared in a new form and even a new nature. We Iranians had become Muslim, like other Muslims. That is to say, in this situation our identity was not only not a refuge for remaining separate, for being ourselves, but on the contrary was the very means of cultural fusion and the elimination of distinction.

But in the sociological arena (and in the process of history), face to face with peoples of the same religion and as a result the "same identity," in particular the Arabs, we still remained a different people with our own identity. From the historical viewpoint Iranian and Muslim, from the social viewpoint Muslim and Iranian, depending on the priority of one's viewpoint, we survived.

In the case of a nation that does not have political independence and is under foreign control, the establishment of a native government, i.e., taking hold of one's own social destiny and digging foundations and building one's history, the situation that developed in Iran in the ninth century, gives shape or form to the nation. National feeling and identity became realizable through the existence of governments. The reason for the existence of the governments was the appearance of the Iranian nation, of "Iranianness."

These governments came about because they were not Arab. From the very start, therefore, they strove to strengthen their own raison d'être and governmental base. And, as already stated, "Iranianness," Iranian national feeling and identity, rested firmly on the twin foundations of language and history. In order to become the wielders of power in their own time, they had to become reacquainted with the past and grasp its reins. This they did. As for language, such dynastic families as the Samanids, Saffârids, Bal'amids, Mohtajids, and Sami-jurids in Khorâsân, Sistan and Transoxiana were both initiators and supporters. They wanted the learned and the eloquent, the poets and writers, to speak and write in Persian. In this fashion Persian writing commenced. Later too, when Turks became rulers, they continued the policy and methods of their predecessors, the Samanids and other Iranian dynasties, in the areas of language and literary culture. With Sebüktegîn, a Samanid general and the founder of the Ghaznavid dynasty, the army fell into the hands of the Turks. With the establishment of the new dynasty, although the army remained in Turkish hands, the administrative system and many members of the court were Persian speakers and made common cause with the new, Turkish-speaking rulers.

A look at the *Târikh-e Mas'udi* [History of Mas'ud ('s Reign)] by Abolfazl Bayhaqi (c. 996–1077)[14] shows that in the period of the Ghaznavid sultan Mas'ud (ruled 1030–1041) the grand chamberlain Bulkâtekin, the doorkeeper Yâraq Taghmesh, the keeper of the harem Boktaghdi, and the regiments of elite troops (Turkomans, Qizil, Buqeh, Kuktash), and confidants of the monarch and those holding court and army positions were Turks. But not only did the army commanders have a Persian-speaking *kadkhodâ*, or staff officer, but also the royal ceremonies of Nowruz, Mehragân and Sadeh were celebrated[15] with the participation of military and government leaders. More important than this was the official status of the Persian language. When the messenger of the caliph in Baghdad presented the caliph's letter to Sultan Mas'ud, the Arabic text was read first and then the Persian (not Turkish) translation by Bu Nasr Mushkam. Documents and letters between Turks and Persians were in Persian, like the letter of Sultan Mas'ud to Qadar Khan, the Khan of Turkestan, or the treaty between Mas'ud and Manuchehr Qâbus, the Prince of Gorgân and Tabarestân (both texts are recorded in Bayhaqi's *History*). The tales of the court of Sultan Mahmud (ruled 999–1030) and his poets are too well known to need repeating. The point is that in general the cultural policy of the Ghaznavid Turks was a continuation of Samanid policy, as was that of their successors, the Saljuqs (ruled 1055–1157). In later periods, other Turks in other lands, such as the Mughals in India and the Ottomans in Turkey, were also lovers of the Persian language and promoted its use in India and Asia Minor. Over the course of centuries, Turkish

---

14. Abolfazl Mohammad b. Hosayn Bayhaqi, *Târikh-e Mas'udi* [History of Mas'ud ('s Reign)], edited by 'Ali Akbar Fayyâz (Tehran), hereafter referred to as Bayhaqi's *History*.

15. *Nowruz* [new day] is the Iranian New Year, celebrated on the vernal equinox, the first day of spring, on or about March 20. *Mehragân* is an ancient Iranian autumnal or harvest celebration. *Sadeh* was a fire festival of ancient Iran.

dynasties and rulers were the means of dissemination of Iranian culture and literature and of our Persian language. Their force ruled us Iranians, while our culture ruled them. Of course the victorious Turks also were aware of their identity and their distinctiveness from the people of the lands they conquered. But not by means of their language, which they did not write and which was not used in the business of state and administration, but rather by military, political, and ideological means: the army, the special relation with the Baghdad caliphate and, sometimes in spite of local populations, their fanatical adherence to the Sunni Muslim faith to which they had recently converted.

Returning to the previous discussion of identity: let me illustrate the special importance Iranians attached to their being Iranian by reference to some Persian poets Asadi Tusi says in his *Book of Garshâsp* (1066):

> Do not shamelessly speak ill of Iran,
> One city of which is better than China.
> What every shah wants of his throne
> Is that his kingdom be Iran.
> Nothing ever arose from Iran except nobility;
> Everyone who wanted a slave bought from among you

The poet Nezami of Ganjeh (d.c. 1205) says:

> All of the world is a body, and Iran the heart;
> No speaker is embarrassed to make this analogy.
> Iran is the heart of the earth; and
> That the heart is better than the body is a verity.

In his famous *qasideh* which begins, "O dawn breeze, if you should pass by Samarqand . . ." Anvari (d. 1190?) mentions Iran numerous times. In this panegyric ode, the poet wants the king to come from Samarqand to Iran (sometimes synonymous with Khorâsân) and save the people from the murderous onslaught of the Ghuzz Turks.

These are examples above and beyond the more obvious evidence of Ferdowsi's *Shâhnâmeh* which show that our poets—Khâqâni (d.c. 1205) in his "Ode to the Palace at Ctesiphon"[16] and Sohravardi (1145–1234) are two others—were well aware of where they were from.

---

16. [MH] Khâqâni, "Ode to the Palace at Ctesiphon," translated and discussed by Michael Hillmann, *Iranian Culture: A Persianist View* (Lanham, MD: University Press of America, 1990), pp. 48-51 and 204-5 (footnote 22).

Religion and Poetry

This study is primarily about Persian prose from a specific vantage point, and not about poetry, which is another subject and a much more complicated matter. But on the question of the relationship between nationality and language, one or two points about poetry deserve mention before returning to our subject proper.

The Koran has no good relations with poetry. A verse in the chapter called "Yâ Sîn" [(the letters) *yâ* (and) *sîn*] states: "And We have not taught him (Mohammad) poetry, nor is being a poet meet for him; it is nothing but a reminder from Allah and His clear word."[17] And in the chapter called "Shu'arâ" [The Poets] appear these verses against poets: "And as to the poets, those who go astray follow them. Do you not see that they wander in the desert of bewilderment? And that they say much that they do not do?" (Koran 26:224–6). The aversion of the Koran to poetry has various reasons. With respect to inspiration and the Koran, the Prophet was most often accused of three things by opponents and those who rejected him: practicing poetry, madness, and gleaning images and ideas from Zoroastrian, Christian, and Jewish scholars and repeating them in the Koran. Of course, responses made to all three charges appear in the Koran.

Prior to the Koran and in the pre-Islamic literary period called 'Jâhilîyyah', poetry was the highest form of Arab discourse, popular and without benefit of reading and writing. Arabs before and after Islam, albeit differently in each age, paid attention to and took pride in their language, its words, pronunciation, grammar and syntax—in short, in building and using it. In the words of the orientalist scholar Hellmut Ritter (1892–1971), their aesthetic was aural: Arab enthusiasm was more incited through hearing, through the ear, and the magic of discourse more quickly enchanted them. The rhythmic and formidable Arabic language in turn encouraged such an inclination in speakers and listeners. On the other hand, the Arabs were a people who had nothing to do with reading and writing. Even in the age of the Prophet Mohammad (c. 570–632), the literate did not exceed a very limited number. Therefore Arab culture was oral, not written. The sum of all these factors caused the extraordinary influence of poetry among the

---

17.   Koran 36:69. [MH] Among many translations of the Koran, the following bilingual American edition has official Twelver Shi'i Muslim approval: *Holy Qur'an*, translated by M.H. Shakir (Elmhurst, NY: Tahrike Tarsile Qur'an, Inc., 1984, third printing). Translations of quotations from the Koran are idiomatic versions of the Shakir text.

Arabs. In any case, whatever the reason, what is indisputable is that they were infatuated with poetry. Poetry was the highest form of discourse, and they had hung the best poems, the seven odes called 'Mu'allaqât,[18] at the Ka'ba in Mecca, which was the house of idols, a place of pilgrimage and commerce, and the holiest of places.

Besides this, practicing poetry was most of the time linked to the priesthood and arbitration. Poetic self-glorification played a major role in display of party spirit, in continuing struggles and tribal conflicts and in their intensification and mitigation. A further relevant point is that the subjects of pre-Islamic Arabic poetry were praise of war, physical love and gratification, and wine. Poetry was oblivious of Judgment Day and sought out the visible world; one can perhaps say that it was primitive and tangible, without moral scruples.

The Koran, which sought to unify the scattered Arab tribes, had set the foundation of the world on Judgment Day. With its new message, it proposed another way of life and also opposed both poetry and the profession of poet. It considered both base and declared the Prophet innocent of both. This negative and suspicious attitude toward poetry remained unchanged for the faithful because it appeared in the Koran. Details left unsaid, the point at issue is that for the reasons cited, religious scholars and theologians always considered the profession of poetry beneath them. They belittled poets and regarded versifying with suspicion. Consequently, although poetry enjoyed widespread popularity in Iran and was ubiquitous, it did not find a place among religious scholars. We have had not only merchant poets and tradesmen and bazaari poets, but even kings who were poets. An example of the latter is the Mozaffarid Shah Shojâ' (ruled 1358–1385) of Shiraz, who in the realm of poetry would rank with—or perhaps a little higher than—Nâseroddin Shâh Qajar (ruled 1848–1896) in his time; in other words, not a mere curiosity. But we never had a theologian poet. Among Shi'i scholars from 'Abdoljalil Qazvini (1110–1189), author of *Kitâb al-Naqz* [The Book of Contravention] to Mohammad Bâqer Majlesi (1627–1699) and later, not one of them had an attachment to poetry, which they sometimes pronounced religiously illicit, indecent, a cause of breaking one's fast, etc. The view of Abolfotuh Râzi (fl. 1087–1131), a leading Shi'i commentator, in his commentary on the verse already quoted from the chapter "Yâ Sîn" of the Koran, is appro-

18. [MH] *Mu'allaqât* [Seven Hanging Odes], translated by A.J. Arberry as *The Seven Odes: The First Chapter in Arabic Literature* (London: Allen & Unwin, 1957).

priate here: "Where it says we did not teach our Prophet poetry, he did not use poetry is a verse in repudiation of those who said that the Prophet, peace be upon him, is a poet and the Koran is poetry. And Â'isha said that poetry was a source of anger for the prophet of God. The Prophet said he had no greater enemy than poetry, and it is reported that the Prophet said: 'If the stomach of one of you is full of pus, I will prefer him to one whose stomach is full of poetry.' "[19]

Despite all of this, poetry later and gradually found its way into religion in the form of popular eulogies, invocations of God, and *ta'ziyeh* dramas (in the realm of folk culture).[20] But in terms of literary value, this poetry was never able to join the ranks of other categories of Persian poetry, especially epic and lyric verse.

The accomplishments of Iranian court figures and Sufi gnostics in Persian poetry are well known. Apart from my earlier comments on nationality and language, poetry was an integral part of court life. In those centuries that are the subject of this discussion and for some time later, the court was the refuge, patron, and customer of scholarship, art, and literature. The much-discussed reasons for this are obvious. Moreover, just as poetry was an integral part of monarchy and court and official administrative life, poets in their turn needed the court, not only for material rewards, i.e., to sell their works, obtain royalties and earn a living, but also for publication of their works. The court and the government were both customers (functioning as the market-place does today) and publishers. In the age of writing by hand and the necessity for scribes, what individual could reproduce a work such as Ferdowsi's Shâhnâmeh? Let's ignore the fact that this great book was indeed transcribed and distributed expeditiously without assistance from the court, because the exception is never a good criterion for judgment. Similarly, a book such as the Masnavi-ye ma'navi [Spiritual Couplets] by Jalâloddin Rumi (1207–1273), for different reasons, never needed the court for publication.[21]

19. Abolfotuh Râzi, *Tafsîr-i rawh al-jinân va rûh al-janân* [Commentary called Garden of Heavens and Spirits of the Heart], 13 volumes, edited by Abolhasan She'râni (Tehran: Ketâbforushi-ye Eslâmiyeh, 1977), pp. 417–418.

20. [MH] Peter Chelkowski, editor, *Ta'ziyeh: Ritual and Drama in Iran* (New York, NY: New York University Press, 1979).

21. [MH] Mowlânâ Jalâloddin Rumi, *The Mathnawi of Jalalu'ddin Rumi*, 4 vols., edited and translated by Reynold A. Nicholson (Cambridge University Press, 1987, first published in 1926).

On the subject of poetry, from this very specific vantage point of
ours, a great number of relevant issues present themselves. For
example, why did Sufi poetry later envelop Persian literature in
general despite the fact it had no connections with and received no
aid from the court? What is the relationship between court and Sufi
poetry in terms not only of content, but also of poetic form? Or how
did it happen that the court, which stimulated the glorious achievements of Persian poetry, later caused its decline and demise?[22] Naser
Khosrow addresses the court poet in these words:

> If you take poetry as a profession,
> Someone has also taken minstrelsy.
> You are standing there where the minstrel sits;
> It is fitting you cut out your impudent tongue.

We know that Anvari thought the nature of the poet was beggary,
and a traveler who came to Iran during the Safavid period writes: "So
that at banquets there might be more means of joy and pleasure, the
Shah pays wages to dancers, female singers, clowns, reciters of epics,
actors, poets, orators, and wrestlers. As for what cloth these people are
cut from, it is better not to discuss it here."[23] Many such questions will
perforce remain unanswered here because they are beyond the purview
of this study.

It will suffice to mention one point on the subject of Sufi poetry.
Gnosticism (*'erfân*) is a sensual experience of the relationship between
the higher world and the self. In the words of a friend, such a deep
experience is rarely expressed in a language other than one's mother
tongue. For example, it would be strange for an Iranian, Persian-
speaking gnostic to sing of his excitement and proclaim the selflessness
of love, the eagerness for union and the pain of separation in Arabic,
a language he learned in school. If such a thing ever happened, it was
rare, and we cannot tell to what extent it was genuine and spontaneous.

---

22. [MH] On the alleged decline of Persian poetry, see Ehsan Yarshater, "The Indian Style: Progress or Decline?" *Persian Literature*, pp. 249–288.

23. Engelbert Kaempfer, *Am Hofe des persischen Grosskönigs*, edited by Walther Hinz
(Leipzig: K.F. Koehler Verlag, 1940) p. 87; Persian translation by K. Jahândâri, *Safarnâmeh-ye Kempfer* (Tehran: Khârazani, 1961), p. 107.

Iranian Governments and the Persian Language

As for writing in Persian itself, these governments faced a problem at least in the matter of religion. Arabic was the language of religion and of the Koran, the prophetic miracle and divine revelation. Iranians accepted the religion. But because they cemented their national identity through language, they were obliged to find a recourse other than Arabic, the language of religion. This led to the translation of the divine word into Persian.

Consider Holy Scripture, the Old and New Testaments, and how long it took for them to be translated into the national languages of the Christians of Europe. It was not only many centuries after the appearance of Christianity, but several hundred years after the appearance of national identity and language. This delay in translating had various causes. One of the most important, however, was the fact that European nationalities were not obliged to take a position in terms of nationality vis-à-vis the language of their religious book and determine a course of action with respect to it. Other tribes had not brought their religion. It had not arrived with war and military expeditions. Their religion did not challenge their nationality. The same held for the language of religion. For us, however, our religion was a part of our identity, but not part of our nationality. We were in a different situation and consequently took another route. We accepted Arabic as the language of God's book and the lofty language of religion, but not as our only language. Persian also became a language of religion. Not without reason were translations of the Koran and Koranic commentaries the first books translated into Persian and among the very first specimens of our prose texts.

The preface to the Persian translation of Tabari's Commentary states:

> "This book is a great commentary by Mohammad ibn Jarîr al-Tabari, may God's mercy be upon him, translated into Persian. They brought the book from Baghdad in forty volumes, written in the Arabic language and with lengthy documentation. It was brought to Amir Sayyid Mozaffar Abu Sâleh Mansur ebn-e Nuh ebn-e Nasr ebn-e Ahmad ebn-e Esma'il, may God show mercy on him and his ancestors. It was difficult for him to read the book because it was in Arabic. He consequently wanted it translated into Persian. So he then brought together the religious scholars of Transoxiana and asked them for a pronouncement that it was legal for us to translate

this book into Persian. They said it was licit for a person who did not
know Arabic to read and write Persian commentaries of the Koran in
accordance with God's words, 'I have not sent any prophet except in
the language of his people.' From ancient times, from the days of
Adam, up to the days of the Prophet Esma'il, all of the prophets and
rulers of the land spoke Persian. And the first person to speak Arabic
was the prophet Esma'il. And this Prophet [Mohammad] emerged
from the Arabs, and this Koran was sent to him in Arabic. And here
in this region the language is Persian, and the rulers of this region
are Persian rulers."[24]

The salient points are that the king wants and gets an edict
(*fatva*) that the Persian language has a history older than the
language of the Koran; that Persian is also a holy and heavenly
language because it is a language of prophets; and that this is Persian
territory here and the kings are Iranian. In this fashion, the door
to translation of the Koran and Koranic commentaries opens and
the Persian language finds its way into the realm of religion.

The lost Shâlmâmeh of Abu Mansur al-Ma'mari was also compiled
in this same period. Its preface is the oldest Persian prose and raises
or illustrates three points. First is the strength of the old writing—
everything about it reaches the nostrils except the odor of decrepitude;
it is alive. Second, it is beautiful; it has a bold and firm beauty. The
third point follows this quotation from the text:

> Praise and thanks to God who created this world and the next and
> who brought us servants into the world and who gave the good
> thinkers and the bad thinkers their due. And greetings to the chosen
> and the pure and religious, especially to God's best creation,
> Mohammad Mostafâ [the chosen], may God's blessings be upon him
> and greetings to the holy family and his children. Here begins the
> work of the *Shâhnâmeh* of Abu Mansur 'Abdorrazzâq 'Abdollâh
> Farrokh who says first in this book that for as long as there have been
> people they have cultivated knowledge, and revered speech,
> considered it the best monument. For by knowledge men are
> rendered more magnanimous and substantial in this world. And
> because people knew that nothing else would remain of them, they
> endeavored that their name might remain and that their repute
> might not fade away.[25]

24. Habib Yaghmâ'i, editor, *Tarjomeh-ye tafsir-e Tabari* [Translation of Tabari's
Commentary] (Tehran: Enteshârât-e Tus, 1977), p. 5.
25. Mohammad Qazvini, editor, *Moqaddemeh-ye qadim-e Shâhnâmeh—Hezâreh-ye*

Because I shall return later to other points in this preface, let this quotation suffice for the moment. The author makes these salient points: for as long as the world has existed, people have pursued knowledge and have held speech in high regard. Here knowledge and speech are synonymous and used together; more specifically they are twins, even one and the same. This is a very ancient notion in the thought and myths of ancient peoples. The beginning of the Gospel according to John reads: "In the beginning was the Word, and the Word was with God, and the Word was God." This "Word" is the translation of the Greek *logos*, which denotes discourse (*kalâm*) or efficient reason and is the world's guide.

In the Christian notion of the Trinity, the second person, the Son, is the very Word made incarnate: "In the beginning was the Word and the Word was with God . . . and Word became flesh." In the Hebrew Bible, Yahweh put himself in the mouths of the prophets of the tribe of Israel, which is to say that what they perceived was the verbal manifestation of Yahweh. In the form of discourse, he appeared among his chosen people and made himself heard.

If the Koran says that nothing exists which has not appeared in that clear book, the reason is that the Prophet brings to it nothing from himself: "Speak in the name of your Lord," says the first verse of the Koran. Koranic verses descended upon the Prophet and flowed through his mouth. The Koran is inspired revelation, which is to say divine discourse; and because it is divine discourse and absolute speech, it contains every science and knowledge, and has everything within itself. Knowledge and speech are linked together.

Of course, the writer or writers of the preface were not seeking to write a treatise on theology. But when we scrutinize their writing today, we can discern a supernatural or metaphysical vision and insight behind the words. At any rate, it is better that we pursue the phrase which is very meaningful in this context: "They have considered speech the best monument." As a monument, speech is something that passed from one person to another, from one generation to another. People in the past leave it for the people in the future; people in the future inherit it from their forebears. In other words, speech is handed down over time, as the substance of history. Not only does history reach us through speech in the narratives of predecessors (just as in the very

---

Ferdowsi [The older preface to the *Shâhnâmeh*—Ferdowsi Millenary] (Tehran: Vezârat-e Farhang, 1943).

Shâhnâmeh whose preface we are reading, they gathered together these narratives and wrote them down, they produced items in the form of written speech so that they might endure and reach people in the future), but also speech itself, insofar as it caused the knowledge of fathers to reach sons, is history, the history of knowing, of awareness.

So that both the knowable things (knowledge) and the memory of a people (history) might survive, and not be spilled like water and vanish, no container other than speech exists in which to preserve it. Speech is the locus where knowledge and history find certitude.

Speech is both the substance of knowledge and the means of transference, i.e., the substance of the perpetuation of its life. Speech has this same link with history, i.e., history is in speech and by means of speech exists and survives. From another vantage point, in order for our disparate information about the world to become a body of connected (organic) known things, to become knowledge, and likewise for these scattered events to be transformed into the memory of a people (history), they must themselves have a life span, they need their own "history."

It would appear that we have now viewed the issue from two viewpoints. Knowledge and history without speech have no subject, while speech as well, which is the bearer of knowledge and history, cannot come into existence without its own "history." With slight oversimplification one can say that knowledge and history constitute the soul, and language the body. That soul in this body enters the world and becomes possessed of form; and this body without that soul has no life. In accordance with this conception, language becomes intermingled, and even one, with knowledge and history.

In any case, in a period when our nationality stood upon the two foundations of language and history, in this preface these two became one cloth and their meaning became welded together, a process that caluminates in the *Shâhnâmeh*.

As for another issue, nothing of a human being endures except for his or her name, and one can preserve that name by virtue of speech, which is "the best monument." A name endures in speech. So Abu Mansur 'Abdorrazzâq, who wants his name to survive, undertakes to use speech. But what is this "speech" that the commander-in-chief of Khorâsân in the midst of all of these transitory things wants to set as an enduring monument to his memory and name? History, i.e., the *Shâhnâmeh*! And that not from his own words and writing, but rather the compilation of the *Shâhnâmeh* at his command. It is as if he would like to say together with Ferdowsi, the poet of Tus: "I will not die henceforth for I am alive / By having cast the seeds of speech."

The preface continues:

> Now the amir Abu Mansur 'Abdorrazzâq was a great and powerful man, cultured and magnanimous, endowed with the will and the means to succeed in all he undertook. He was ambitious and of a mighty lineage, that of the *sepahbads* [the military aristocracy] of Iran. He had heard of the translation of *Kalileh and Demneh* by order of the king of Khorâsân [Nasr ebn Ahmad the Samanid] liked what he heard. He wished of fate that there might also be a monument to him in this world. So he commanded his minister Abu Mansur al-Ma'mari that the possessors of books, such as the lauded gentry and the learned and the widely traveled be brought from the provinces. And at his command his servant and steward Abu Mansur al-Ma'mari wrote a letter and sent it to the cities of Khorâsân to summon the wise, such as Siyâj son of Khurasani from Herat, and Yazdandad son of Shâpur from Sistan, and Mahuy Khorshid son of Bahram from Neyshâbur, and Shâdân, son of Barzin from Tus. He had brought together all four of them, and set them to work on this Book of Kings: to record their deeds and lives, the days of justice and injustice, tumult and war, cults and customs, from the first Keyanian ruler who introduced human customs into the world and distinguished human beings from animals, down to the time of the Sasanian monarch Yazdagerd III, the last of the non-Arab kings. This he did in the month of Moharram in the year 346 of the hijra (957 C.E.), and called it the *Shâhnâmeh.*

So, Abu Mansur 'Abdorrazzâq Tusi is a man "of the sepahbads of Iran" and "of a mighty lineage," in other words, has roots in a distinct past, that is, possesses history. This "historical" man, like those knowledgable ones from the cities of Khorâsân, is possessed also of a historical consciousness. That "he wished of fate that there might also be a monument to him," i.e., aware of the roots he has in the past, he longs for branches and leaves in the future. A "conscience" and historical self-awareness, thoughts of continuity, voyaging from one place to another, is obvious in his desires. He does not want to be a meaningless and forgotten link in a continuum without the characteristic of time. He wants consciously to link the past, which has meaning and is history, to the future, so that the future likewise will not be without meaning. In short, he wants to have a meaningful place in this temporal voyage. He is a "historical" man with historical awareness who wants to connect past and future through the mediation of his own personal existence. Of course, the discussion here is about perception of history, not about the accuracy or inaccuracy of facts. As a result, whether or not Abu Mansur 'Abdorrazzâq is really from an old family has no bearing on the discussion. If his name and particulars are counterfeit, it makes no difference from our vantage point. Counterfeit history is itself a historical phenomenon when it answers a cultural or social need. In the words of the literary historian Zabihollâh Safa: "Determining the lineage of kings and princes was necessary because there was no Sultan or claimant to the throne of Iran in the ninth and tenth centuries who did not trace his ancestry somehow or other to ancient kings and heroes."[26] Thus, in order to rule in Islamic Iran during this period, a connection with pre-Islamic Iran was a prerequisite. In any case, Abu Mansur 'Abdorrazzâq was a man from an old family who wanted a monument of his person to remain. He is a man who wants to endure in history. He turns to speech, and his speech, the *Shâh-nâmeh*, is history. The affairs and lives of Iranian monarchs from the first mythological ruler to the Sasanian king Yazdagerd III are the history of his own people. There, speech and history had become one. Here, a person becomes historical through speech.

A short time later, another great man from the same region of Khorâsân repeats with a slight difference the work of Abu Mansur 'Abdorrazzâq. I refer to the historian Bayhaqi, who says: "My aim is to write a basic history and to build a great structure such that mention of it will remain until the end of time."[27] The first works of Persian prose—this preface to the *Shâhnâmeh*, Bal'ami's History (completed in 962), the translation of the Koran, and Tabari's Commentary commissioned by Mansur b. Nuh (ruled 961–976), and a theological treatise by Abolqâsem b. Mohammad Samarqandi (d. 953)—are about history and religion, the two grounds of our nationality and identity. Except for the treatise, the three great works were completed at the behest of princes and through the efforts of viziers (the court and governmental establishments).

To sum up, if we turn to such first-hand histories as the History of Sistan (11th century) and History of Bokhara and take note of the behavior of the conquering Arabs, especially in Khorâsân and Tran-

---

26. Safa, *History of Literature in Iran*, vol. I, p. 218.

27. *Târikh-e Bayhaqi*, edited by Q. Ghani and A. Fayyâz (Tehran: Enteshârât-e Gâm, 1945), p. 96. Hereafter referred to as Bayhaqi's *History*.

soxiana, in converting people to Islam, collecting the kharâj tax, and their governmental methods, we can better sense the awakening of national feeling that I have discussed in such detail. In the awakening of this feeling, the conquering people had an essential role. All of this sketch I have outlined of the national and cultural mentality of that age is one-dimensional and incomplete, and at best illuminates only a dim corner of the truth. National feeling or even national awareness is just one of many divers visible and invisible factors of history. If we cast a superficial glance from another angle, we will see how other, even contrary, factors were influential, and how from this twisted and jumbled skein the current that we call the history of Iran in certain centuries came into being. In the tenth and eleventh centuries, the Baghdad caliphate began to weaken. Throughout the empire, numerous regional governments freed themselves from their ties to Baghdad, among them in Iran the Tâherids, the Samanids, and the Saffârids. About the same time or a little later mention should be made of the Ziyârids, the Buyids, and the 'Alids of Tabarestân. Despite a shared opposition to the Baghdad caliphate, most of these dynastic families fought among themselves, to the consequent benefit of the caliphate, over the extent of their realms and royal power. For example, The Samanid Esma'il fought with Mohammad b. Zayd who had revolted in Tabarestân against the 'Abbâsids. On the one hand, he was destroying an enemy of the caliph; on the other, despite the caliph, he advanced westward to Rayy and Qazvin. Examples of this sort are numerous. In relation to the Baghdad caliphate, contrary to the clash between Ya'qub the Saffârid and the caliph, there was not always, as Bayhaqi observes, a consistent policy. Asad (son of Sâmân Khodhat, the founder of the Samanids) had four sons. The 'Abbâsid caliph Ma'mun (ruled 786–833) gave each of them a governorate over a principality. He gave Samarqand, Ferghâneh, Châch, and Herat respectively to Nuh, Ahmad, Yahyâ, and Elyâs at the beginning of the ninth century. They ruled on behalf of the 'Abbâsids, even though they were at the same time the first national dynasty, the first Iranians to rule over Iranians in the Islamic era. But, from another angle, Ma'mun's partiality toward the Samanids and other leaders of Khorâsân (and toward the 'Alavids, when he declared his successor to be the Imam Reza) was not unrelated to the dispute between Ma'mun and his brother Amin over the Caliphate and the decisive part to be played by the armies of Khorâsân.

This series of events, although tangential to our subject, shows us how winding, twisting and intertwined are the roads of history, and how misleading it invariably is to grasp one or two strands and judge them without reflection.

The Government Establishment and Persian Prose

Issues of nationality, language and history naturally brought the first works of Persian prose into our discussion. Now we can turn to the contexts to which members of the court and government paid the most attention, contexts in which either they themselves or their associates did the writing, either on their own initiative or with the encouragement of others, and with various aims and purposes. The phrase "members of the court and government" denotes not only those who had a rank, position, or duty in the royal court or agencies of the government, but also those associated, directly or indirectly, temporarily or permanently, with the governmental institution who could write and whose products and services the government purchased, from astronomers and geometricians to physicians, geographers, secretaries and historians. Court prose can be classified in general under the categories of history, social-didactic essays, science (astronomy, medicine, pharmacy, and the like), geography, official correspondence, philosophy and ethics.

Here, for various reasons, I will talk only about the first two categories from a single, specific perspective. First and foremost, in a brief monograph one can hardly say anything about one thousand years of prose. Secondly the other categories are mostly works of technical prose, which are interesting from perspective of the study of technical terms, lexical combinations and linguistics in general, or the history of science, the evolution of prose, cultural and social history; but for our purposes, the linkage of prose writing with national feeling, they are indirect and of secondary importance. Furthermore, readers of technical prose were an elite group familiar with technical prose, which could not enjoy a wide circulation. On the other hand, such categories as court and administrative correspondence (secretarial prose of scribes) were not only generally influential in the evolution of Persian prose, but also—for reasons we need not go into, having more to do with Iranian court politics and customs—later played a leading role in the decline and corruption of Persian prose. In any case, despite the extraordinary importance of philosophical and scientific prose, and the works of such leading figures as Avicenna (980–1037), Biruni (973–1050), Naseroddin Tusi (1200–1274), Qotboddin Shirâzi (d. 1365), and Baba Afzal (c.1190–c.1260)[1], I can deal only with history and social-didactic treatises. In history as well, my focus is more on the interpretation of history, not on the quality of historical prose, which itself naturally deserves a lengthy and technical discussion and investigation. In addition, I will focus on the relationship between historians and the court.

The Historians' Conception of History

We had two sorts of history in the first period: on the one hand, the *shâhnâmeh*s and, on the other, such formal histories as Bal'ami's History, the *History of Sistan*, the *Summary of Histories*, and Bayhaqi's *History*. The existence of these two sorts of histories presumably bespeaks two different conceptions of history and two different cultural and political roles we Iranians expected history to fulfill.

On the subject of the *shâhnâmeh*s, two points deserve to be added to what has already been said. Except for the thousand couplets by Daqiqi (d.c. 980) and Ferdowsi's *Shâhnâmeh* (c. 1010), the other *shâhnâmeh*s have unfortunately not survived. But, from the treasure that has survived, in that period the *shâhnâmeh*s or, to be more exact, myth-

---

1. [MH] E.g., Naseroddin Tusi, *The Naserean Ethics*, translated by G.M. Wickens (London: Allen & Unwin, 1964).

ological-heroic histories of Iran (whether oral or written), were a means of preserving our national memory. The spiritual and shared past, the historical culture of every people, is the basis for linking its individuals to one another. Such works transform people from separate individuals into members of one single whole. The *shâhnâmeh*s exercised for us the function of this past and simultaneously living culture. The *shâhnâmeh*s preserved within themselves the memories of the Iranian people, which also constituted the wellspring of shared feelings. A nation without memories is like a man without a memory. These *shâhnâmeh*s did not allow us to remain like old men without a past, like people without lineage, confused between past and future. They gave us a place in time and space. In contrast, although the formal histories of Bal'ami and others spoke of non-Arab kings, their conception of history and their primary function were something else.

As for the second point, insofar as one can judge on the basis of Ferdowsi's *Shâhnâmeh*, Daqiqi, Abu Mansur's Preface or Asadi Tusi's *Book of Garshâsp*, and such surviving Sasanian epics as *Ayâdgâr i Zarêrân* [The Chronicles of Zarêr] and *Kârnâmag i Ardeshir i Pâpakân* [The Gesta of Artakhsher, Son of Pâpak], these histories embodied in their own way the Iranian world view. Not only in the mythological sections, in the great stories of heroes, but even in the stories of the Sasanian monarchs, the coronation speeches and their feasts and battles, one can see a picture of good and evil, the world and the hereafter, a concept of God and man, the customs of administering the country, social relations, and many other things. The world view of a people found a place and became embedded in a history which was constructed and nurtured over hundreds of years from prehistoric times. (I have treated these two aspects separately in order to make my point perfectly clear. Otherwise, they are fundamentally identical, and the memories and world view of a people coalesce at the foundation.)

Now let us turn to the formal histories and their conception and perception of historical writing. The first thing that comes to mind is that from the advent of Islam in Iran during the 640s to the beginning of the Constitutional Movement (1905–1911), our historians shared some general (and I emphasize general) conceptions and perceptions.

The Religious View of History

In this period, for example, the historian's conception of history and of human social affairs is religious. God created the world in the course of several days. With the creation of the world, time and, following that, "history" begins. Because the world was created, it has a destiny which needs to be fulfilled at the Resurrection. Resurrection Day is the end of history. Human social affairs also have a place in this general ordering of existence. As the noblest of creatures, man can have a fate superior to that of angels or lower than that of devils, according to his faith and actions. But in any case his life is not separate from the course of the world, and divine will is at work in all of his states and actions. As another illustration, the birth and death of each person—that is, his beginning and end, which is to say, the history of his life—is known and certain beforehand. For human social affairs as well, which were visualized as the numerical aggregate of individuals, a similar view existed. In this fashion, the motivating force of history, that which encompasses society, is not within society itself but rather is from the supernatural world and corresponds to divine will. At the same time, it should be noted that the discussion is of change from one state to another, and not of progressive evolution, going from one stage to a higher stage, because the concept of historical evolution is a later phenomenon and has no relevance to the age under discussion.

On this matter, Bayhaqi says: "When Almighty God created man, He so arranged his fate that sovereignty was constantly transferred from this people to that people and from this group to that group. The best testimony for what I am saying are the words of the Creator Himself, may His glory be glorified and His names be sanctified, Who said: "Say: O Allah, Master of the Kingdom! Thou givest the kingdom to whomsoever Thou pleasest and takest away the kingdom from whomsoever Thou pleasest, and Thou exaltest whom Thou pleasest and abasest whom Thou pleasest; in Thine hand is the good; surely, Thou has power over all things" (Koran 3:25). Therefore, one must understand that there is a divine wisdom in Almighty God's taking the shirt of a king from one group and putting it on another group and a universal good for men on the earth which surpasses man's understanding, such that no one can imagine why this is so, much less explain it."[2]

---

2. Bayhaqi's *History*, p. 98.

Bayhaqi wrote this in the invocation to his *History* where he wants to explain the general principles of his view of history, just as he talks also about his own two historical models and paradigms: Alexander and Ardeshir, one a monarch of the Greeks and the other a king of Iran, both considered founders of great empires and history-makers. Because Bayhaqi is writing secular, not sacred history, he chooses his two models from among kings, not from among prophets.

Divine Will in History

Now, the movement of history depends upon divine will. Not a leaf falls from a tree unless it is God's will. But divine will is not knowable. Human beings are unable to comprehend it. Therefore, in practice and in general, history is not a matter of reason in this sense that human intelligence neither established it nor has an essential and general role in its development; because human beings are not the cause of history, but rather the means for the realization of divine will. In other words, history is a given decreed from above. On the basis of this conception, Islamic historians view human social life as equivalent to the destiny of individuals and groups, a destiny in which human beings have no say, whether in constructing the framework or sketching the outlines. Because history stems from divine will and because it is non-logical, we consequently confront many problems which are part of, and accepted as, history, but which cannot be explained through criteria of logic and reason. (Sometimes the writers themselves have been aware of this and have reminded their readers of it.) Most histories begin with the fall of Adam and proceed to the monarch of the moment or the age of the author. It was customary for history to begin at the very same place where myths and stories began. Myths were a part of history and were accepted without question (which is the business of logic and reason) because rational criticism in today's sense of the word had no place in history. In this fashion, the stories of the Companions of the Cave (the Seven Sleepers of Ephesus), 'Ad and Thamud, Joseph and Zolaykhâ, and Koranic narratives in general, were not only part of historical writing, but constituted the most meaningful parts of it and its paradigms. In this context, such historians as Bal'ami or the unknown author of the *Summary of Histories*, who were Iranian and Muslim, endeavored to effect harmony between the mythological history of their own people and the Koranic narratives. As a result, they identified Zoroaster with Abraham and paralleled Jamshid and

Solomon, or, for example, compared the story of Varjam the Kurd with Noah's storm, and equated Kayumars and Adam, or, in Bal'ami's words, "Mashya and Mashyâna, whom the Muslims call Adam and Eve."

Our official historiography begins with Bal'ami's translation of Tabari's History, the original title of which is a telling indication of the author's aim: *History of the Prophets and Kings*. Its history of the prophets is from Adam to Mohammad, the Seal of the Prophets. Its history of the kings treats the monarchs of Iran. In addition, like the translations and commentaries of the Koran, the Persian translation was executed on the order of the Sasanian ruler Abu Sâleh Mansur b. Nuh (ruled 961–976) by Abu 'Ali Mohammad b. Mohammad b. Abdollâh al-Bal'ami (d.c. 974?), the vizier of Khorâsân. Iranian scholars wrote the originals of these books in Arabic, while other Iranians translated them into Persian.

However, Bal'ami's work is not just a translation. He added to the original, expanded it, made it more comprehensive. For this reason, it is better known as Bal'ami's History. In any case, Bal'ami says in his preface:

> When I looked in it [Tabari's History] and saw much scientific knowledge, evidence, Koranic verses, good poetry, and much that was beneficial, I toiled and strove, and with the help of Almighty God forced myself to translate it into Persian. I wanted to record in this book the history of the ages of the world as observed by everyone from astronomers on, including members of all peoples who have composed history, Zoroastrians, Christians, Jews, and Muslims, whatever each group has said. And whatever I did not find in the book of Jarir's son [Tabari], from the days of Adam to Resurrection Day, I added to it in order, God willing, to make it comprehensible and easy to read.

This history of the world finds its bearings with citations of Koranic verse. Bal'ami begins with the creation of the world and Adam and proceeds not only with Koranic guidance to describe the course of history, but also invokes the verses of God's book here and there. These are what guarantee the accuracy of the material and the correctness of the work, and not the gathering, scrutiny, and comparison of documents and other data which comprise the basis of historical writing today. Because of this different conception of history, Bal'ami's method of historical writing also was different. These Koranic verses, like links in a chain, tie together the events and happenstance of past ages.

History as the History of the World

History is the history of the world, not just the narrative of human society. Because the creation of the world and that of man was approximately simultaneous, and because the world was created essentially for man, the noblest of creatures, history is the history of the world and man, which makes the words of the astronomer as relevant as those of the historian. In fact the historian here wants to record a description of the lifetime of the world "from the days of Adam to the Day of Resurrection," from the creation to doomsday. Because he does not find this in Tabari's account under the heading "Revealing the History of the World According to Every Statement of How It Is and Shall Be," he searches for other evidence in the words of Aristotle, Hippocrates, Plato and other masters. After quoting them concerning the beginning and end of the world, the author-translator Bal'ami, and not Tabari, introduces material from the myths of Iran. He introduces the view of Ibn al-Moqaffa' on "the grand *shâhnâmeh,*" the words of Mohammad b. al-Jahm al-Barmaki, Zâduyeh b. Shâhuyeh, Bahram-e Mehrân Esfahâni, the accounts of the Sasanians and of the kings of Pârs and Farrokhân-e Mobadân, the priest of Yazdagerd, and other knowledgeable people so that he might present the fortunes of the world from beginning to end.

Moreover, in those lines quoted from the book's preface, primary importance lies in the Zoroastrian and Muslim nature of the topic, as I stated in the discussion of identity, not in its Iranian or Arab nature. But the fact that the Muslim author, despite the Koran, presents the statements of others, and with particular emphasis on the statements of Zoroastrians, and sees in them knowledge, wisdom and benefit, shows that interest in peoples and nations of other religions had been stimulated and awakened. Other people, among them the Magi, had said things about the history of the world which, like the statements of Muslims, were useful. The history of other Iranian groups counts and is of value. Out of caution and in order to avoid misunderstanding, I shall say no more on this matter.

In any case, the writer does exactly what he claims: the "histories" of Zoroastrians and Muslims are brought together and proceed in parallel fashion. He begins with a brief treatment of the Zoroastrians and then deals with Islamic history: the creation of the sky, the moon, the stars and the earth, Satan and Adam, heaven, the garden of Eden, the fall of Adam and his landing in Ceylon, and the narrative of Cain and Abel. It is as if he is collating and arranging the Koranic stories in chronological order. Then he returns again to Zoroastrian ideas about the creation of the world and Adam: Kayumars and Hushang, the Divs and Jamshid, Zahhâk, and the dynasty of Pishdâdian. He then proceeds to the end of the myths of both peoples side by side. In this fashion the historical personalities (and, implicitly, beliefs) of the Iranians before Islam find a rightful place and are naturalized among the Muslims.

In contrast to the *shâhnâmehs*, which dealt exclusively with the "history" of Iran, the official histories from Bal'ami to Gardizi (fl. mid-eleventh century) and the *Summary of Histories* and other histories describe in parallel fashion the Iranian and Arab peoples. They make compatible and harmonious the past of the two peoples so that one (the myths of Iran) approaches the sacred status of the other (Koranic narratives), or at least the past of one (Iranians) achieves the same acceptability as the other (Arabs). An example is Gardizi's *Zayn ol-akbâr* [Selected Annals] (1049–52), which begins with Tahmuras and Jamshid. After the Kayâni dynasty and kings of tribes (Arsacids) come the Sasanian kings and the Chosroes. The sixth chapter cites the histories of the caliphs and rulers of Islam.[3] As another example, *The Summary of Histories* (1126) has the following order: history of the prophets, history of some non-Arab kings, history of the kings of Byzantium, history of the Arab kings and the predecessors of the Prophet. The *Fârsnâmeh* [Book of Fârs] (1111) of Ibn Balkhi likewise deserves mention as an example of the so-called "short" books of history or regional geography. It treats the Pishdâdian, Keyanian, Ashkânian (Arsacids), and Sasanians.[4] At the same time we should recognize that the source of most of these histories is the works of such great figures as Tabari (d. 932), Mas'udi (d.c. 952), and Hamza al-Isfahâni (c. 893–c. 961), historians who wrote the history of Iran and the Arabs, Zoroastrians and Islam, in Arabic. These writers, intentionally or not, display an intelligent conception of the reality of the existence and coexistence of the two peoples, the Arabs and the non-Arabs.[5]

---

3. [MH] Abu Sa'id 'Abdolhayy b. Zahhâk Gardizi (11th century), *Târikh-e Gardizi* [Gardizi's History] or *Zayn ol-akbar* [Selected Annals], edited by 'Abd al-Hayy-e Habibi (Tehran: Châpkhâneh-ye Armaghân, 1984).

4. [MH] Ibn al-Balkhi, *Fârsnâmeh* [Book of Fârs], edited by Guy Le Strange and Reynold Nicholson (Tehran: Donyâ-ye Ketâb, 1984, second printing).

5. On the blending of Iranian and Arab legends and the justification of pre-Islamic Iranian beliefs in these early Islamic histories, see Arthur Christensen, *Les types du*

In any case, to return to the subject of histories written in Persian, their cultural and social role was not limited to curiosity and learning about the past, as in the case of the *shâhnâmehs*. And historical writing or even counterfeiting of history (as observed in the case of creating family trees for some dynasties) was not just a means for achieving political and social aims. The past was a matrix, a basis on which to stand, where a people might find their own abode in time (i.e., their own place in the "present") in order to know where in the temporal scheme of things they are, in their own words "the fortunes of the world." In other words, knowing history is connected with finding one's niche in the world.

On the other hand, these histories reconciled the past of the two groups to make possible their equality and coexistence and for them to find actuality. These historians are the interpreters of the national feelings of a conquered people who accept the religion of the conquering people, but not their government. They resist accepting the latter's political and racial superiority and are not prepared to be second-class citizens (Whether willingly or not does not have a primary significance for reasons beyond the purview of this discussion.) Thus, if the role of the *shâhnâmehs* is to stimulate national feeling by awakening the memory of a people, the official histories serve to reconcile the national issue with the religious issue. In their attempt to achieve harmony with the reality of the time and to seek for a middle road, remaining Iranian and being Muslim, these histories functioned in a way similar to the Sasanians in the realm of politics and government. Perhaps it is a reflection of that same mentality and conception in the realm of culture. These histories and these *shâhnâmehs* both take advantage of similar sources and raw materials with respect to the history of Iran, but each with a differing aim and result.

The Model for Historical Writing

As already noted, Koranic narratives were the paradigm and model par excellence for historical writing because the Koran naturally provides the best advice on the philosophy of God's work. Although divine will is not comprehensible to human beings, at the same time no divine action is lacking in wisdom. God does nothing useless or

---

premier homme et du premier roi dans l'historie légendaire des Iranians (Stockholm, Norstedt, 1917–34).

in vain. Moreover, He has sent prophets and guides and likewise inculcated human beings with reason. Therefore everyone can, and should, in his own way derive guidance from God's wisdom and distinguish the path from the pit. And that is precisely what the Creator expects from the created and reminds him of.

There is a difference between divine will and the wisdom of God's actions. Will is put into action on account of the wisdom which inheres in it. In actuality, will is a form of cause, and wisdom an effect, a result, or an aim, although literally the work of God does not admit of cause and effect. The willing of it and its execution are simultaneous and identical. The order of cause and effect pertains to created human beings. If we analogize, it is out of necessity for purposes of explanation. Otherwise, from another perspective, the comparison of the action of the Creator and created is an analogy with a distinction. Be that as it may, God's will is set in motion for the wisdom which inheres in it. The human race must learn by example from the guidance of those sent (prophets) and God's wisdom as it manifests itself in human society (in history). If the human race cannot find a way to understand the motive (will), it cannot comprehend the result and find the way to salvation. From this perspective, Koranic narratives are a model for historical writing. In such a situation, the aim of historical writing is the exposition of divine will, the explanation of peoples' destiny and fate so that they might learn from those who have gone before. And heeding lessons means perceiving the wisdom of God's actions to the best of one's own ability and good fortune and consequently becoming compatible and in step with divine will (in other words, faith and works).

Koranic narratives in fact are warnings and reminders: O you who believe, know that individuals or peoples who disbelieved, ignored the will of God and behaved according to their own will, were destroyed. If you have any doubt, hear what happened to Pharaoh, Nimrod, Qârun, 'Ad, Thamud, idol worshippers and the others. In contrast, those who were obedient to the will of God and did not forget God in toil and misfortune were ultimately saved, like Abraham, Jacob, Joseph, the Virgin Mary, and others. In the words of Sa'di:

> Because Noah's son sat with evil doers,
> His family's prophetic mission was lost.
> Whereas the dog of the Companions of the Cave for a few days
> Followed the doers of good and became ennobled.

The Iranian historian in the Islamic era has such a pattern in mind and emulates that same Koranic aim. As a result, the historian who has no more expressive model or criterion than the book of religion for heeding lessons, for learning the way of life and eternal salvation, instinctively returns to religion. The philosophy of this historical writing is religious. That is to say the life and soul of the lower, mundane world is in the upper, heavenly world. It is the desire for that world which gives meaning to this world, to what transpires here, to the chaos and ups and downs of people's lives.

Mention here of Ibn Khaldun (1332–1406) might be useful. Everyone knows his famous *Muqaddimah* [Introduction].[6] He is that rare Muslim historian who utilizes rational and logical criticism in understanding reports and assessing historical events so as to distinguish between fact and fiction. In Ibn Khaldun's view of things the important issue is that human society and individuals undergo change as a consequence of natural, climatic, cultural, economic and other causes. The moving forces of history are social realities and natural phenomena, regional conditions of desert and city life, and climate. Their effects in the disposition and customs of peoples is the leaven for the creation of civilization and consequently for changes in the way of life of individuals. History is the arena of the development of societies. But despite all of this, in the twenty-fifth chapter of the first volume of the *Introduction,* we see that ultimately, in the best government, the country must be administered with the guidance of Islamic law and on the path of eternal salvation. Like other historians, Ibn Khaldun here and there invokes Koranic verses to support arguments and to add emphasis to conclusions. In this fashion, a meticulous and comparativist historian such as Ibn Khaldun is not without a model for interpreting history in his style of writing it. At the same time, the full title of the book introduces its aim. His history is a book of lessons in the continuous chain of events: *Kitâb al-'ibar wa dîwân al-mubtadâ' wa al-khabar fî ayyâm al-'Arab wa al-'Ajam wa al-Barbar* [The Book of Lessons and Compilation of Subject and Predicate on the Times of the Arabs and non-Arabs (Persians) and the Berbers].

---

6. [MH] Ibn Khaldun, *The Muqaddimah: An Introduction to History*, 3 vols., translated by Franz Rosenthal (Princeton, NJ: Princeton University Press, 1967, 2nd edition).

Other Motives in Historiography

The commentary above deals mostly with the context of the philosophy of history-writing. Behind every first-rate book of history lies
such a philosophy, more or less, witting or unwitting. These were
the historian's aims and abstract, ideological ends. But in writing,
historians had other, perhaps stronger and more influential motives, personal and social motives related to practical, daily life.
When a vizier such as Bal'ami or Rashidoddin Fazlollâh (1247?–
1318) or 'Atâmalek Jovayni (1226–1283), who were in the center of
the political and governmental life of their age, takes up history-
writing, it is obvious that he also has more practical and tangible
personal and social aims than heeding warnings and finding the
straight path to heaven. These other aims relate to their social position and their relationship with the court and the government establishment. Historians were usually either members of the court
and government or dependent on them, directly or indirectly,
which even a cursory look at some famous Il-Khânid and Timurid
historians will show.

    Hendushâh Nakhjavâni, the author of *Tajâreb al-Salaf* [Past Expe-
riences], was an agent of the government and governor of Kashan.
'Abdollâh b. Fazlollâh Shirazi (1264–1334), who under his title Vassâf
al-Hazra was the author of *Vassâf's History*, was a land-tax adminis-
trator. Hamdollâh Mostawfi (fl. 1330–40s), the author of *Târikh-e
gozideh* [Selected History] was from a family of accountants and secretaries and a tax collector. Sharafoddin 'Ali Yazdi, the author of
Zafarnâmeh-ye Taymuri [Tamerlane's Victory Record] (1924–25) was a
companion to the Timurid monarch Shahrokh (ruled 1405–1447) and
his son Ebrahim Soltân. Kamâloddin 'Abdorrazzâq Samarqandi (1413–
1482), the author of *Matla'-e sa'dayn va majma'-e bahrayn* [The Rise of
the Two Auspicious Planets and the Confluence of the Two Seas], was
in the service of Shahrokh and the Timurid princes. Mir Khând (1433–
1498), the author of *Rawzatossafâ* [Garden of Purity], had Mir 'Ali Shir
Navâ'i (1441–1501) for a patron. Khând Mir (c. 1475–c. 1535), the
author of *Habibossiyar* [Beloved of Biographies], was also a protege of
'Ali Shir Navâ'i.[7]

7. [MH] Hamdollâh Mostawfi, *Târikh-e gozideh* [Selected History], edited by
'Abdolhosayn Navâ'i (Tehran: Entershârât-e Amir Kabir, 1983, first published in
1960); translated by E.G. Browne and R.A. Nicholson (Leiden, 1912). 'Abdollâh b.
Fazlollâh Vassâf al-Hazra, *Tahrir-e Târikh-e Vassâf* [Redaction of Vassâf's History], by

These are examples from a period in which the writing of history flourished. But the historian's social position and extreme dependence upon princes and governors precipitated the decline of historiography, while the defense and praise of the actions of despotic sultans and sycophancy (in the works of some historians in the employ of the court) led to the neglect of professional honor and pertinent ethical considerations and, in general, the search for truth. *Zafarnâmeh-ye Taymuri* states that Tamerlane (ruled 1370–1405) seized Isfahan and commanded that whatever horses and weapons there were throughout the city should be turned over to the "servants of the Mars of vengeance." The city's elders and leaders had an audience with Tamerlane and, to assure their security, accepted the cost of taking care of the victorious army. They divided the city up and appointed officials and agents and apparently put so much pressure on the people that a rebellion ensued in 1388, in the course of one evening of which three thousand people were killed. Now note the tone of the historian: "The next day when they informed the blessed ears of the monarch as to the nature of the event, the fire of his world-engulfing anger flamed and he ordered the victorious army to sack the city." Each of the leaders is charged with gathering a certain number of chopped-off human heads. Soldiers unable to kill the city's defenseless people with their own hands bought severed heads in order to meet their own quota, first at twenty dinars a head; then when everyone had accumulated his share, the price of each head dropped to half a dinar. The writer adds that it was reported that at least seventy thousand heads had been chopped off in Isfahan, out of which they had built towers of skulls at numerous sites.[8]

This historian on the payroll of Tamerlane's son records such tragedies as if he were talking about miracles of saints. The profession of such a historian is not historiography but flattery, without which he cannot support himself. In other periods as well appear instances of similar sort. The tone of *Summary of Histories* on the conquest of Rayy by Mahmud of Ghazna, the murder of the leading citizens of Daylam and other people, and the burning of tons of books of the Râfezis

'Abdolmohammad Âyâti (Tehran: Enteshârât-e Bonyâd-e Farhang-e Iran, 1967). Mirkhând, *Rawzat al-safâ*, translated by E. Rehatsek as *The Rauzat-us-Safa, or Garden of Purity* (London: Royal Asiatic Society, 1891).

8. Nezâmoddin Shâmi (fl. 1392), *Zafarnâmeh: Târikh-e fotuhât-e Amir Taymur* [Record of Tamerlane's Victories], edited by Panâhi Semnâni (Tehran: Sazman-e Nashr-e Ketâb, Enteshârât-e Bâmdâd, 1984).

[Twelver Shiites] and Bâtenis [a branch of Isma'ilis] is not empty of praise and glorification.

It must be noted that a historian who lives under the autocratic government of a Tamerlane, or a Mahmud, even if he does not taste "Asiatic despotism" for himself, at least has his hand on the fire from a distance. In addition, he believes the verse which reads: "Say: O Allah, Master of the Kingdom! Thou givest the kingdom to whomsoever Thou pleasest and takest away the kingdom from whomsoever Thou pleasest, and Thou exaltest whom Thou pleasest and abasest whom Thou pleasest; in Thine hand is the good; surely, Thou hast power over all things" (Koran 3: 25).

The Safavid Shâh Tahmâsp I (ruled 1524–1576) put it this way in his own autobiographical chronicle:

> O you who have struggled after good fortune,
> Fate and fortune are not the fruits of skill.
> Whoever has position and wealth and glory
> Has it only because of heavenly grace.

He is a monarch who considers himself sovereign and his kingdom deriving from heavenly grace; and he justifies his actions on this basis, like the author of the *Zafarnâmeh* and those bizarre deeds of Tamerlane. In the invasion of the Mongols, many people said that Muslims were facing divine wrath, because they were unable to account for that terrifying and "illogical" event in any other way. In any case, only the rare historian in such periods was bound by ethical aims and theoretical issues. The writing of history was an administrative occupation for the worldly Mammon. But insofar as the historian lives in an Islamic cultural environment, the "philosophy" of that religious perspective just discussed finds its way willy-nilly into his writing. However, in periods of social and moral decline, that same "philosophy" in the hands of jaundiced and sycophantic historians (who unfortunately were not, and are not, few in number) becomes transformed into a means for justifying and even praising murder and cruelty.

History and Ethics

References to ethical considerations call into play the subject of ethics and value judgments in history. If written for the edification of readers, history must accept good and reject evil. The issue of good and evil (ethics) thereby presents itself. These are "moral" histories in this sense, that a morality or a kind of admonition lies hidden in them. The historian's view and understanding derive from the religious and ethical world. Therefore, even when he does not have them in mind, religious and ethical conclusions practically ooze from his writing, because history wants to teach right conduct and the right way of life, to prevent readers from straying onto the wrong path and losing this world and the hereafter. In this sense, no gradations or distinctions appear. In the genesis and texture of nearly all of our histories, morality lies at the heart of it; in fact every age has its ethics, bound up in the cultural and non-cultural condition of the age. For example, the ethics of *Nâsekh al-tavârikh* [Abrogator of Histories] by 'Abbas Qoli Sepehr (1851–1923) differs from that of Bayhaqi's *History*. Look at the pretentiousness of the title: a history that has no need for other histories, because it is their abrogator—no trace here of the humility of the seeker after truth! The book itself is also not very scrupulous in terms of truth.Thus, concerning the assassination of the Qajar vizier Amir Kabir in 1852, the narrative tends toward mollifying the murderers rather than telling the truth. Bayhaqi records the assassination of Hasanak, and Movarrekh-oddowleh Sepehr that of Amir Kabir, a similar event. But there is a world of difference between them, and a great ethical distinction between the two is obvious in the descriptions of these two events.

The transmission of ethics in history is a matter both of self-awareness and of instinct. Drawing ethical conclusions, providing guidance and here and there pointing out pitfalls to the reader is a task the historian permits himself, quite contrary to the nineteenth century and after, when Western historiography changed. The study of facts, documents and reality, free of any sort of value judgment, the historian's remaining apart from the history he is writing, the method that was employed in the study of nature and experimental sciences, the objective method, became customary as well in the writing of history. We Iranians also later adopted this method. It is obvious that in this view of history and in this method of writing history, no place remains for the expression of personal opinion, lessons for living and ethical teaching, or for the expression of feelings. Today these thrusts in the writing of history are unacceptable and diminish the scientific value of a work. But in the past, for the very reasons already cited, the historian exhibited no reluctance and sometimes insisted on expressing personal views in those contexts where he deemed it necessary, in the matter of religion or ethics. And because the writer considered these personal views the results and products of history, and the goal, and point to the citation of events and occurrences, sometimes the events constituted a mere preface for reaching this end. The expression of opinion could have for him an importance greater than "scientific exactitude" and recording and cataloging events. Of course, for such leading historians of ours as Bal'ami, Bayhaqi and Rashidoddin Fazlollâh, exactitude in the recording of events and dedication and fidelity to reality, and consequently to truth, are an essential matter even when their aim is deriving morals or lessons from events, because such are prefatory to that advice and the wisdom of history; and one cannot reach a correct conclusion from a disordered and confused introduction. But in any case if attention to events did not lead to the discovery of wisdom hidden in them, it would be defective and incomplete, like knowledge without action.

Attention to External Appearances

Because "scientific realism" did not have primary importance for the Iranian historian, his original and chief interest likewise was not drawn to the causal connections among events. Rather he devoted his attention more to that which derived from events and happenstances. That is to say, his attention was more attracted to phenomena that seemed the products and results of events that were factors of the first order in influencing social life, or were imagined as such. In this sense the historian was less concerned with forces hidden in the heart of society that are factors in historical development than with external and visible manifestations of the development, i.e., the rise and fall of a dynasty, the relationship of kings and viziers, or war. More often than not, war itself or blatant clashes that result in war are the subject of history, not the social, economic, geographical, and cultural causes that manifest themselves as war. Such history highlights the exposed sore or cancer, but not the germ hidden in the body which surfaces as a sore.

For example, our first-hand histories in Persian and Arabic that discuss the Arab invasion of Iran usually do not treat in detail social and class structure, relations between government and people or between classes or the role of religion, social and moral decay, the heavy burden of taxation, poverty, oppression and the like—all factors toward the end of the Sasanian Era which caused such a great empire to collapse so easily. Not that such things go unsaid, but they are said less often. On the other hand, "foreign affairs," the surface manifestation of something going on underneath attracts greater attention, for example, the battle of Jalulâ, the battle of Nehâvand (642), the slaying of Yazdagerd in 651 by the miller, military campaigns and conquests.

At the same time, we should not forget that if the Arabs come to Iran and bring a new religion, the Muslim historian views this change as resulting from divine will. The religion of Mohammad must prevail and God's creatures must accept God's religion. If toward the end of the Sasanian era (224–651), things had been better, if corruption and social and cultural decay had not existed, the result would still have been the same in the Muslim's historian's view. If divine will had determined upon bringing Zoroastrians into the flock of Islam, it would have been realized regardless—this view of history has its own sort of historical determinism.

Of course, if conditions were different, divine will also would have been implemented in another form. But for the Muslim historian, the principle is the advent of Islam, not the form of its advent. Thus, searching for prior causes the result of which would be the form of the advent of Islam in Iran and the form of the fall of the Sasanians is a secondary matter for the historian, as indeed it was. See what Bal'ami says about the end of the Sasanians: "Almighty God wanted to take this kingdom from them and to have it become Muslim; and he thus confounded them."[9]

It is not only the destiny of nations and religions that are controlled from the world above, but also individuals. An example is Bayhaqi's representation of the final words of the vizier Hasanak before his death in answer to Abu Sahl Zawzani, who had called him a "Carmathian dog." It is a long and very interesting story, at the end of which Hasanak says: "I do not know who is a dog. My family and what is mine by way of trappings and wealth and status, all people know. I enjoyed the world and accomplished things and at the end of a man's career is death. If death is to arrive today, no one can hold back the gallows or any other doom, for I am not greater than [Imam] 'Ali's son [Imam] Hosayn."[10]

Death is predestined. Despite all of the sultan's power and the powerful life of the court and the games of the age, death arrives on

---

9. Bal'ami's *History*, p. 1209.
10. Bayhaqi, *History*, p. 184.

its appointed day, just as Imam Hosayn's death arrived. Early or late, death is beyond one's control. That which is at work in bringing life to a close comes from somewhere else. It is divine will. With such a view, the interest of the Muslim historian in perceiving the cause of things, their original cause, besides the earth, also naturally focuses on heaven. He does not see all cause and reason here. Consequently he does not expend all of his energy and intellect in searching for mundane and social phenomena, causes, and motives.

The history of the Ghaznavids offers another and final example. The historians of that age, in treating Mahmud's military expedition to India—he himself called them *ghazavât*, i.e., in the tradition of the Prophet, the wars were for the propagation of Islam, and other such high-sounding pronouncements make no mention of the method of conscripting soldiers, their numbers, the effect of conscription on the economic situation of cities and villages and other such events. More than anything else is the hue and cry about Islam, the accumulation of reserve forces, conquest and such things as attract attention. Scrutiny of social or cultural phenomena, if it occurs, comes from a rare or unique scholar such as Al-Biruni (c. 973–1048) in *Tahqiq mâ lil-Hend* [Alberuni's India] or *Al-Âthâr al-bâqiya'an il-qorûn il-khâliya* [The Chronology of Ancient Nations], not from writers of history.[11]

The long and the short of it is that when the causal and hidden connections of events in historical development are less noted and investigated, the principal role falls to grand political and military events which take place in the realm of the monarchy and the court and government organization. At the same time, these events are better and more appropriate for the conclusions the historian wants to reach about politics, administration and ethics, and for the lesson he wishes to communicate to the reader.

Perhaps this has been one reason why, for political and military history, the comings and goings of dynasties, wars, and such, have received the bulk of attention in our classical historiography. Of course, numerous other causes, simple and more obvious, have also existed from the very beginning. When a historian is dependent upon the court or government and leads his material and spiritual life on the

---

11. [MH] Al-Biruni [Abu Rayhân Biruni], *The Chronology of Ancient Nations: An English Version of the Arabic Text of al-Âthâr . . .*, translated by Edward Sachau (Lahore, 1982, first printed in 1879); *Alberuni's India*, translated by Edward Sachau, 2 vols. (London, 1882).

basis of this relationship, willy-nilly and in accordance with his occupation he must fulfill obligations in compensation for what he receives, for God does not give anyone rations or salary.

Here one must also bear in mind that the indifference of the Iranian historian to the output of hidden, latent forces and his attention to external, blatant events is not just a matter of inattentiveness to the former and ready service to the latter. Judgments of this sort come easy and pat, but they are not fair; they are the products of lazy minds. The discernment of these "internal forces" is a modern notion born of the human sciences in recent times. The curiosity of historians or researchers in past centuries, in any case, was not capable of progressing beyond limits, the limits to truthfulness, awareness, and personal diligence. It was not possible to carry out the investigation of a great number of social phenomena and relations systematically and methodically. These phenomena and relations were still unknown.

The Mongol Period

The Mongol khans were a model of despotic cruelty in governing and administering Iran. Nevertheless, their age was one of the most brilliant periods of Persian historical writing. Among the various reasons for this fact I will cite two or three that relate more to the role of government in the writing of history.

The Mongols were desert-wandering, tent-dwelling tribes with an oral culture and a simple social organization. After conquering Iran and settling there, they confronted a progressive, extensive civilization and culture, and a people with a court, a religious and educational system, and an economic and commercial order which differed greatly from their own. The Mongols became the ruling class in this kingdom. Their language, religion, customs, style of life, and social and governmental structure differed from those of the local people. Aware of this situation, they maintained these differences for some time. They convened their own tribal and governmental *qurultay* or council every few years in Mongolia and preserved as much as possible their relation with that center and their family connections. Into their hands had fallen the government of extensive lands, which they wanted to keep for themselves. Of course they employed Iranians as viziers, courtiers, tax collectors, magistrates and policemen. But all of these were appointees of the Khan and functioned as his agents, not as his colleagues.

Theoretically, legally, and even in terms of common law, these Iranians were granted no rights or shares for themselves in government. The Khan recognized that he had come from another place and was ruling over another people or peoples. For this reason, however much he might employ local people in court tasks, everyone in the army, the princes and military commanders, and the military administrators were Mongols. The army was composed of relatives of the Khan, of people from his tribe.

In order to keep the government in their own hands, the Mongols endeavored for some time, that is for as long as they were not attracted and absorbed into Iranian society and culture, to remain separate from the governed, from Iranians. In other words, for them as well the issue of identity was at stake—but for different reasons and characteristics from those of the Iranians in the past: the Iranians to escape from subservient roles and to gain rights for themselves, and the Mongols to maintain their own authority and to keep in their own hands the prerogatives of others.

The Mongols also turned to their own history to protect their identity. Probably for two principal reasons, the Mongol khans paid special attention to the history of their own tribe and people. The history of the tribe has an essential importance for families who have control over other individuals and tribes of other people. In the tribal system, in whatever form it may be and mixed with fables, tales, and myths or truth, this "history" justifies the legitimacy of the ruling family. The family that is older, larger, and possessed of a lengthier ruling tradition theoretically has more rights to rule over others.

Moreover, after their arrival in Iran the Mongol khans paid much attention to the history of their own people as a whole, a ruling people, a people separate from the local population, especially since they had invaded and settled among a people who had an ancient history and a luxuriant culture. Consequently, the Mongol khans paid great attention to the history of Mongolia, the Mongol people, and the family of Chingiz Khan. They encouraged historical writing and facilitated the completion of such a great work as Rashidoddin Fazlollâh's *Jâme' al-tavârîkh* [Compendium of Histories].[12] Several of the best Persian books are the products of this period, among them

---

12. [MH] Rashidoddin Fazlollâh (Tabib), *Jâme' al-tavârikh* [Compendium of Histories]; translated by J.A. Boyle as *The Successors of Genghis Khan* (New York: Columbia University Press, 1971).

Târikh-e Jahângoshâ [History of the World Conqueror] by Jovayni (1226–1283)[13] and *Compendium of Histories*. As far as we know, the latter is the most comprehensive and most important Mongol history written during the period.

Now, the authors of these two histories were rulers or viziers and not on the fringes of the court, as were other historians. Being close to the monarch, in all likelihood they wrote their works at his behest or suggestion or at least with his approval. In addition, the Mongol khans were not Muslims to start with. For example, in the case of *The History of The World Conqueror*, the shah of the day, Hulagu, was not Muslim. In the case of *Compendium of Histories*, Ghâzân Khan (ruled 1295–1304) was a recent convert to Islam. Therefore the authors were to a great extent free of religious (= Muslim) and ethical constraints. Their religious world view finds its way into their works, but mostly subconsciously. And insofar as concerns conscious awareness, i.e., general moral didacticism, the historian does not insist (in *The History of The World Conqueror* the Isma'ili "Assassins" appear more as political and social enemies than as philosophical opponents). Instead, the emphasis of the leading historians in this period is on the events. In terms of an inclination toward the truth, gathering useful information and honesty of reportage, the histories of this period are superior. Even the duplicitous *Vassâf's History* with its frightful language contains information not often found in Persian histories. Another point deserving mention is that during this period the khans either did not know Persian or knew just a little. Consequently, verbal artifice and pedantry on the part of a writer, however dependent upon the person of the king, did not influence the latter greatly. Therefore the positive and negative qualities of the language of these works and the distinguishing characteristics of their prose bear directly upon the history and sociology of the language. Their good and bad qualities derive from themselves and not from their connection with the court.

Of course, I have referred here only to general factors influential in historiography. But perhaps even from these generalities one may conclude that historical writing in any given period can be studied in terms of the history of that period. Information about the general perspectives of the historians (as treated in the first part of the discus-

---

13. [MH] 'Atâmalek Jovayni, *Târikh-e Jahângoshâ*; translated by J.A. Boyle as *The History of the World Conqueror*, 2 vols. (Manchester: Manchester University Press, 1958).

sion), although necessary for understanding the work of historians, is not sufficient.[14]

Social-Didactic Literature

I shall now treat another sort of prose by members of the court, for lack of a better term here called "social-didactic" writings or works. To clarify my purpose, I have to return to the distant past, to Iran before Islam. If we look at the writings that have survived from that period, we can distinguish in general three literary types: religious literature, historical-epic literature, and social-didactic literature.

The *Bundahishn* and *Dênkard* [Arts of Religion] or *Zand i Vahuman Yasht*, *Ardâviraf-nâmag* can be cited as examples of religious literature.[15] It is true that these works were collected and compiled at the beginning of the ninth century to preserve them from the ravages of events and the times. But because the texts were religious, hence sacred, and because their compilers were *mobad*s, that is, men of religion and presumably believers, one can imagine that they at least did not alter the surviving works on purpose and that they preserved them as they were, so far as they were able. Furthermore, after the Arab conquest and the advent of Islam, Zoroastrians became encapsulated groups, and the Zoroastrian faith, which had become a stagnant religion of a minority under pressure, evolved very slowly. As a result, one can surmise that extant works, even though compiled three centuries after the collapse of the Sasanian empire, are representative of Mazdayasnan religion and the way of thought and religious outlook of the Sasanian epoch.

This part of Pahlavi literature finds its way into the Islamic era, that is, into Persian literature, and in the seventh century reaches the Zoroastrian Bahrâm Pazhdu. He was a helpless and ill-fated poet because he was Zoroastrian, because he was part of the quiet and subdued group of Zoroastrians of Rayy; the culture of those unfortunate people

---

14. Manuchehr Mortazavi, *Tahqiq dar bâreh-ye Dawreh-ye Ilkhânân-e Irân* [Research on the Il-Khânid Period in Iran] (Tehran: Ketâbforushi-ye Tehran, 1962), p. 153, counts thirty-three Mongol histories and concludes that the quantity and quality of histories during the days of the Mongol Il-Khanids, i.e., from 1252 to 1340, is the direct result of the encouragement of this art by the Mongol rulers or inspired by the general renaissance of historiography in this age.

15. [MH] On Zoroastrian religious literature, see Dale Bishop, "Literary Aspects of the Avesta," *Persian Literature*, edited by Ehsan Yarshater, pp. 41–56.

could not achieve any brilliance in those days of prejudice and cruelty, and their literature was clandestine. Bahram Pazhdu himself was a third-rate poet who, whenever he could, justifiably deplored their sad plight. This thread of literature does not catch on in Islamic Iran; it cannot play a role until it comes to life. That which remained concerning the religious concepts of Mazdayasnâ has a secret, trans-formed life and raises its head in another guise from other places.

On the subject of epic-historical literature, we know that after the advent of Islam it soars and reaches its pinnacle in Ferdowsi. The roots of this branch of Iranian literature reach back, on the one hand, to the *Avestâ* and Iranian mythology and, on the other, to the Arsacid Period (250 B.C.E.–224 C.E.) and the epic and fabulous history of that epoch. This literature, with the lengthy Sasanian era behind it, reaches Ferdowsi already with many developments and changes, and attains its final fixed form after hundreds of years in his words. In this sense we differ from the Greeks, whose epic achieved its final form at the beginning, that is, probably after three or four hundred years. I shall not go into detail here because others have done so and because I have referred to the matter elsewhere.[16] Our epic tradition has a long history.

Of history-epics at the end of the Sasanian age, we are familiar with *Khodây-nâmag* [Book of the Lords/Kings] which was also translated into Arabic, but of which at present nothing has survived except for citations here and there. The *Kârnâmag-i Artakhsher-i Pâpakân* [The Gesta of Ardashir Pâpakân] or, for example, *The Chronicles of Zarêr*, are extant and a perusal of them can lead one to surmise about the ways in which the people of that age viewed history.

Then there is the third sort of writing, social-didactic literature. Here my interest lies in this final type which has been chiefly expressed in the form of compendiums of advice, aphorisms, folktales and short pieces. The substance of these writings is social and moral; it is the practical wisdom of forebears and the teaching of their experiences to others. This branch of literature likewise continues after the advent of Islam and grows strong again and more fruitful in the soil of Persian literature. *Kalileh and Demneh* (although its origin is not Iranian), *Qâbus-nâmeh* [A Mirror for Princes], *Siyâsat-nâmeh* [The Book of

---

16. [MH] Shahrokh Meskoob, *Moqaddemeh bar Rostam va Esfandiyâr* [A Preface to 'Rostam and Esfandiyâr'] (Tehran, 1964), and *Sowg-e Siyâvash* [Mourning of Si-yâvash] (Tehran, 1971).

Government], and *Chahâr Maqâleh* [Four Discourses] are prominent
examples.[17]

First of all, and to avoid any possible misunderstanding, I should
state that my interest is exclusively in the content of these works, not
in their form. It is obvious that, with its language of animals and
stories of Indian origin, *Kalileh and Demneh* does not resemble the
straightforward, erudite, and dry exposition of such works as Nezami
'Aruzi's *Four Discourses*. Even in terms of content, the difference
among these works is not slight. They are related and similar to one
another only in the several respects that led me to discuss them
together in the category of social-didactic works.

The Writers of Social-Didactic Essays

The authors of social-didactic essays are usually members of the court.
I use this categorization, as mentioned earlier, in the broadest sense,
to refer to those who have a court occupation, those dependents with
duties, and people nearer to the court in social and cultural terms than
to others, not only those to whom Sa'di refers as "nurtured on the
bounty of the great." As an example, let us take Sa'di himself (c. 1215–c.
1290) who was not only not the dependent of a prince or vizier or the
scribe at some court, but was not even bound for much of his life to
any city or region. Nevertheless, when he was in Shiraz, he dealt with
the Atâbegs, even if by way of offering advice to the king in *qasideh*s. I
do not want to talk about social and class rank because that phrase is
trite as a result of constant, narrow, and inappropriate use. In the case
of a person such as Sa'di, it is also confusing. Nevertheless, if we
examine his social situation from this angle, he is not a shopkeeper,
tradesman, craftsman, or city bazaari, nor a villager or merchant, nor
a religious elder or jurisprudent or Sufi, although he is a sermonizer
who utilizes pulpits. In social terms he is at the upper limit of those
endowed with culture and knowledge who are connected with the

---

17. [MH] The most recent translation of Ibn al-Moqaffa's *Kalila wa Dimna* is *Kalileh
and Demneh: An English Version Based on Ancient Arabic and Spanish Manuscripts*, translated by Thomas Ballantine Irving (Newark, DE: Juan de la Cuesta, 1980). Kay Kâ'us
b. Eskandar b. Qâbus, *Qâbus-nâmeh* [Book of Qâbus], translated by Reuben Levy as
A Mirror for Princes (London: E.P. Dutton, 1951). Nezâmolmolk, *Siyâsat-nâmeh*,
translated by H.S. Darke as *The Book of Government* (London: Routledge & Kegan
Paul, 1960). Nezami 'Aruzi, *Chahâr maqâleh* [Four Essays], translated by E.G.
Browne as *Four Discourses: Revised Translation of the Chahâr Maqâla* (London, 1921).

leaders of government and the establishment, despite the fact that he is not literally a government agent or official.

Just as the writers are from a specific group, the readers of these works likewise are not everybody, although it is true that *Kalileh and Demneh* and Sa'di's *Golestân* [Rose Garden] (1258)[18] achieved general popularity. More typically, Nezâmolmolk's *The Book of Government* or Kay Kâvus's *A Mirror for Princes* addresses a limited audience or a small group, because the subject is essentially not useful to everyone. Someone like Nezâmolmolk would not care to make available to ordinary people the methods of managing the subject population and the state. In *Four Discourses*, Nezami 'Aruzi writes his rules of secretaryship for people of culture.

The Topics of Social-Didactic Essays

The subject of these works is another of their shared aspects. In general, like earlier advice books, they deal chiefly with managing the country, controlling matters of property and the people, the rules and forms of government, practical philosophy, and ethics and social behavior. It is a very broad subject area, encompassing most of the arenas of social and cultural life, but not all of them. They deal with social, ethical, and cultural life in accordance with the inclination and taste, and from the viewpoint of groups who are involved in or at least interested in managing society, i.e., the administrators rather than the administered.

The point is not to denigrate these works to the level of political-propagandistic writings and to say that, for example, they were deliberately written for the perpetuation of the government of one class over another. Such superficial statements signal the forced comparison of today's political ideologies with past culture. But I do want to say that politics, culture, ethics and, in general, "social affairs" as they appear in these books have naturally been seen from an elitist viewpoint, although very often with some breadth of vision. I do not want to say that they are colored by elitist self-interest, because that is an inappropriate conception insofar as it brings to mind only

---

18. [MH] Sa'di, Golestân, edited by Gholâmhosayn Yusofi (Tehran: Enteshârât-e Kharazmi, 1989); translated by Edward Rehatsek as *The Golestan or Rose Garden of Sa'di*, edited with a preface by W.G. Archer, introduction by G.M. Wickens (London: George Allen & Unwin, 1964). Quoted material from Sa'di's *Golestân* appears here in adaptations of Rehatsek's translation.

economic profiteering, power-seeking, and riding herd over others. It might be better to say that these books embody the source and substance of elitist policy preferences, with all the positive and negative features which became accepted over the course of centuries as the advisable course for the generality of people, and received general approval. Let me cite an example from the poet Hafez (c. 1320–c. 1390): "O cupbearer, pour wine in the cup of justice so that the beggar / Will not rise in defiance, to fill the world with calamity."[19] This couplet is simple enough not to need explanation. It would be difficult to express in fewer and clearer words the aim of justice behind *Kalileh and Demneh* or, for example, *The Book of Government*. I use this example because of its expressiveness. Hafez is normally not a good example because his ethic has different roots and derives sustenance from another source. One can also cite as a shining example Sa'di's anecdote in *The Rose Garden* of his argument with a man who was antagonistic to the wealthy, especially since in this dispute Sa'di sides with the wealthy, not the poor. The interpretation of "those endowed with authority" in the Koran, and of kingship and the relationship of sultan and subject in these works, is another indication of the social views and beliefs of the writers of these works.

Common Characteristics of Social-Didactic Essays

Another common feature of these treatises is their prose, their language. What I say here about this aspect is true also about histories.

Today a person who writes in the humanities or literature has an unspecified audience. His or her aim is to establish contact with an unknown and disparate audience belonging to varied groups and social strata. What has emerged since literacy became widespread in modern societies is known as a "market." Usually (I emphasize usually, without regard to special circumstances, which are quite common) a book is a commodity written for the market; and the reader buys it like any other commodity. The relation between writer and reader, if it exists, is through such mass media as the press, radio and television. Because writing is a commodity, the issues of merchandising, the publisher's business, author's royalties or fees and a thousand other things obtain.

---

19. [MH] *Hafez, Dance of Life* (Washington, D.C.: Mage Publishers, 1988), offers two English versions of twelve representative *ghazals*, along with an afterword which treats the Hâfezian ethic.

Today, when what a writer says is for the public, not for a group of intellectuals or the like, usually his language approaches the mass language, to the point of sharing in the language of the whole audience, not for instance the special idiolect or jargon of a particular group or profession.

In the past, things were otherwise. The author of *The Book of Government* or *A Mirror for Princes* or even *Kalileh and Demneh* did not confront such people as his audience, nor did he think about contact with them. The writer belonged to a specific social group. Either he was in the court or government or somehow connected with them, or he wrote at the behest of the king, a vizier or a prince. Or if he wrote with the thought of publication, he dedicated his work to them. Literate people were not numerous. A literary market or market for books did not exist. Books were not commodities. Author's fees, publishers and the like, none of them was involved. The customer, publisher, and fee payer was the "organization" of the court and civil administration. (Religious and gnostic groups were also, though in a different way, the customers and publishers of their own works; this I shall treat later). The audience for these works was likewise not large. The literate segment of the population were intellectuals and, more often than not, close to the writer in social terms, or at least not far from him. They were not the general public.

In past society, established levels and patterns existed in regard to education and knowledge. In our religion, tradition was a pillar of theology, law and rights, ethics, and worldly and spiritual behavior. In contrast, innovation in religion was tantamount to apostasy. Social and family life was based, through a series of levels or degrees, on the relationship between sultan and subject, master and apprentice, man and wife, father and offspring. Everything had its own special pattern, ways and customs—in a word, tradition, the sum total of which constituted the rules for living, that very entity today called "culture." A person acquainted with the rules or a person of letters was a person of culture. Poetry and other writing also had their own rules. A court poet or clerk or accountant usually had to proceed through stages from apprenticeship to mastery. He would learn the craft and skills of poetry and secretarial work—prosody, rhyme, rhetoric, figures of speech and the rules for clarity and eloquence. Subsequently he would put into practice these approved and relatively enduring laws. In the treatises under scrutiny as well, the particulars and rules of writing were observed, which is to say that all of them are literary, as are the bulk of the histories. In other words, people of erudition wrote eruditely for people of erudition, sometimes without pedantry as in *The Book of Government* and sometimes pedantically as in *Kalileh and Demneh*. Sa'di's *Rose Garden* is the rare example of erudition that is pleasant and not annoying. Generally, in periods when the language was healthy, literary devices served as decoration and rhetorical embellishment. But in eras of decline, the substance of discourse suffocated beneath the onslaught of prolixity and pedantry.

A Glance at Sa'di's *Golestân* [Rose Garden]

For reasons already stated, the language of all of these social-didactic works is literary Persian. The appearance of vernacular prose in literature relates to another time, when the populace enters the political life of society and counts for something. Learned language—not in the pejorative sense, rather in the sense of language the writing of which is learned, as it were, like a science–reaches perfection in Sa'di's *Rose Garden*, to the point where, for example, the whole preface serves as a perfect specimen of eloquence in Persian prose and a model for later writers. Interestingly, in the longest and most important narrative in *The Rose Garden*, the story of Sa'di's dispute with a man who opposes the wealthy, the conflict between the parties is resolved and the judge's decision accepted when the latter brings rhetorical skill to its limits. In other words, the magic of discourse brings the dispute to a close: "When the judge brought speech to this limit and rode the steed of hyperbole beyond the limit of our ability to analogize, we acceded to his judgment, and let bygones be bygones."

On the style of *The Rose Garden*, Mohammad Taqi Bahâr (1886–1951) asserts that Sa'di had the *Maqâmât* [Rhetorical Anecdotes] of Hamidi (d. 1164) in mind in writing the book, but discarded the latter's use of Arabic, rhythmic prose, and wearisome rhyming.[20] One can add that the aphorisms and wise sayings at the end of *The Rose Garden* are reminiscent of the final chapters of the Koran in terms of eloquence, succinctness and pithiness. But our interest here is basically on the

---

20. Mohammad Taqi Bahâr, *Sabkshenâsi, yâ tatavvor-e nasr-e fârsi* [Study of Style, or The Evolution of Persian Prose], (Tehran, 1958), vol. 3 p. 125. [MH] A short English sample of *Maqâmât-e Hamidi*, begun in 1156, appears in E.G. Browne, *A Literary History of Persia*, vol. 2 (Cambridge: Cambridge University Press, 1969, first published in 1906), pp. 348-9.

subjects and content of *The Rose Garden*, in which are crystallized Pahlavi literary saws together with practical wisdom of our culture's Islamic periods. It is sociology in the sense of care of the state's subjects and managing state affairs, teaching ethics and social behavior, customs, the transfer of experience of forebears and elders to others (which in a traditional, conservative society means the transfer of culture) both indirectly, through tales with morals and directly, through admonishment. The conclusion of Sa'di's masterpiece bespeaks its author's purpose:

> I have given advice here in my own manner,
> And spent a lifetime in the task.
> If it should not please anyone's ear,
> Messengers are accountable for their messages, nothing more.

The chapter divisions of *The Rose Garden* also imply the most essential categories of the culture and social ethics of Islamic Iran. The book has the following eight chapters: On the Character of Kings, On the Morals of Dervishes, On the Virtue of Satisfaction, On the Advantages of Silence, On Love and Youth, On Weakness and Old Age, On the Effects of Education, On Rules of Social Life and Friendship. First is monarchy, and opposite it is the way of the dervish. Then comes the way of the dervish in everyday life (contentment with one's lot), in thought and speech (silence) in the world of despotic sultans. The fifth and sixth chapters are social-ethical observations about humanity which, contrary to their titles, have little to do with age or youth. The seventh chapter is more about the lack of influence of education than about its effects. The eighth and final chapter is a summary and extract of the whole book, most of it in the form of aphorisms and short wise sayings, the fruits of practical philosophy, under the telling title, "Rules of Social Life."

In Iranian society, one party was the king, possessed of prerogatives, and the other party comprised subjects devoid of social rights. These two categories, in every imaginable guise, the government and the people, are naturally the most important topic of these social-didactic works. It so happens that in this regard as well, Sa'di's *Rose Garden* would appear to be the quintessence and culmination of this whole social and didactic belletristic tradition, especially from the perspective of succinctness, expressiveness and clarity. At the end of Sa'di's argument with the man about the wealthy, the judge's speech ends with mention of the qualities of the monarch of the day, the atâbak Abu

Bakr Sa'd-e Zangi. The king is only "the seeker of name and forgiveness and possessor of this world and the next." And then:

> No father ever treated his own son with as much generosity
> As the hand of your magnanimity has done to the family of Adam.
> God wished to show mercy to a whole world;
> In His mercy He made you the world's monarch.

It is after this that Sa'di and the man with whom he argued become friendly: "They bow their heads in deference to one another and kiss each other's head and face." Sa'di here alludes to the father-son relationship of the king (of course in his view a just king) with his subjects. As for relations among subjects—the rich and the poor—it is likewise alluded to in the precept's last two couplets, which in fact are their whole upshot:

> Do not complain about how the world turns, o poor man,
> For you will be unfortunate should you die with this view.
> And you, o wealthy one, since your hand and heart have their fill,
> Enjoy and be generous—you have won here and hereafter.

Sa'di's practical philosophy lies in the establishment of a father-son relationship between king and subject and a mutual justice between rich and poor for the purpose of achieving peace and reconciliation in social life. In his view the proper course for society and its participants lies in this reconciliation. His ethics consists in planning the proper social course. The point of departure and heart of his ethics derives from this.

Two Sorts of Ethics

When we look in the most general terms at Iranian belles-lettres after Islam, we essentially confront two ethics. One is the ethics which continues from *Kalileh and Demneh* to *The Rose Garden* and works written in imitation of it. The structure of this ethics is based on social prudence or expedience, and on Sa'idi's maxim, "the politic lie is better than the truth which upsets things." In like fashion, consider the social ethic of *Kalileh and Demneh*, behavior that is necessary in life and daily actions: frustrating the machinations of others and keeping one's own goods dry. We see the other features of this ethical and behavioral stance in such works as *The Book of Government* or *A Mirror for Princes*.

However, alongside this are other works by those engaged in the business of government in which we see another ethics based not on social prudence, but on deeper and broader foundations. It is founded not only on a conception of social relations, but also on a conception of the relation of man with heaven and the whole world. This ethics is not mindful of prudence or expedience, but of truth. It is not social but, as it were, cosmic, celestial, and general. The preeminent examples are the ethics of Ferdowsi's *Shâhnâmeh*, Bayhaqi's *History*, and in a sense Hafez's poetry. I say "in a sense" because one end of Hâfezian ethics touches gnosticism, which is another issue altogether. In any case, the culmination of this second ethical voyage is in Hafez, just as the first finds its culmination in Sa'di's *Golestân*. Afterwards both enter a decline, just as the glory of our literature reaches its nadir in "ethics"—or at least in the manifestation of ethics in belles-lettres something along these lines happens.

Not only do the aforementioned writers possess a different kind of morality, but the subject matter of their work is also different, even though they too are engaged in the business of government in the broader sense of the term. To return to *The Rose Garden*, the literary language or the literary role of social-didactic prose works reaches its culmination in Sa'di's book. Because the perfection of speech, especially in Classical literature, was attained in poetry, *The Rose Garden* not only embodies metered and in this sense poetic prose, but also prose and verse intermingle and blend throughout the book. In my view, the success of the language of the book was not just that it later became the model for men of letters. Fascination with and unqualified acceptance of the language of *The Rose Garden* also brought equally unconditional acceptance of Sa'di's social ethics as well. Of course, because social and historical factors for the acceptance of this ethics were in place as well, men of learning approached the book with such approval and praise that they did not proceed to exercise critical judgment of its ethics. Sa'di's language implanted Sa'di's ethics as well in men's minds and there fixed them. The numerous imitations of the style and expression of *The Rose Garden* testify to its later deep influence. Two of the most famous are the *Bahârestân* [Spring Garden] by Jâmi (1414–1492) and *Parishân* [Perturbed] by Qâ'âni (1807–1853), which belong to two completely different periods.

Discussion of this ethics here draws to a close because *The Rose Garden* is the pinnacle of one sort of prose writing. Rhythmic and rhyming prose intermingles with verse, "versified prose" with content

from practical philosophy. For this reason *The Rose Garden* is like
Hafez's *Collected Poems*. The latter does something with the *ghazal* verse
form from which no poet thereafter can escape. That model is
evermore present. One had to equal or surpass it, which was not
possible. Or one had to be satisfied with imitation, which was undertaken out of necessity. It took hundreds of years before another route
opened for Persian poetry. *The Rose Garden* likewise did the same thing
to this species of prose (although not to all prose). After it, writers
became slaves to imitation.

The Period of Return in Prose

From the end of the Safavid period (1501–1736) a new interest arose
in ancient verse and prose, mostly in the Khorâsân style in poetry, from
Sorush (d. 1868), Neshât (d. 1828), 'Abdorrazzâq Beg Donboli (d.
1827) and others onward. M.T. Bahâr rightly calls it a period of return
(*bâzgasht*). No resurgence or renaissance took place, but rather a partial
return to origins. As for prose, Bahâr's view is that the plunder of the
libraries in Isfahan by the invading Afghans, likewise the dispersal of
library collections in Delhi and Bokhara and especially the sale of these
to buyers in Shiraz, followed by a thirty-year period of security, tran-
quility, and prosperity during the reign of Karim Khan Zand (ruled
1751–1779) permitted literate Iranians to become acquainted with
illustrious works of Classical Persian literature which had fallen into
disfavor during the Safavid era and were no longer being read or
taught, which brought about a change in taste among the educated.[21]

For this historical reason, as well as other social and purely literary
causes, court prose—by turning to pre-Safavid models—entered a
new phase from the Zand and the early Qajar periods. For example,
again in his *Study of Style*, Bahâr describes Donboli's writing style as
something between that of Jovayni, Vassâf, and Sa'di. He considers
Donboli's *Tajrebat al-Ahrâr va Tasliyat al-Abrâr* [Experience of the
Noble and Consolation of the Pious][22] to be a masterpiece of the early
nineteenth century, possessing all of the positive characteristics of past
technical prose characteristic of a literary resurgence and a return to
the Classical style. He likewise considers Neshât's style as between

---

21. Bahâr, *Study of Style*, vol. 3, pp. 316–19.

22. [MH] The only sample of 'Abdorrazzâq Donboli's prose in English is a different
work, *The Dynasty of the Kajars*, translated by Harford Jones Brydges (London, 1833).

Vassâf and Sa'di, and cites an unpublished essay of Neshât's composed in the manner of Sa'di's *Rose Garden*.[23] Imitation of *The Rose Garden* reaches its zenith with Qâ'em-maqâm Farâhâni (1779–1835), but does not end there. In his *Monsha'ât* [Literary Compositions], he comes closer than others to Sa'di's style. In the view of 'Abbâs Eqbâl, Sa'di's *Rose Garden* was the model for the language of court scribes throughout the Qajar period.[24] In addition, until the Constitutional period (1905–1911) and even for a time thereafter, it was not only the premier textbook of Persian language, but was also in effect our most important Iranian text of practical philosophy. Even a cursory glance at the works of nineteenth-century writers shows the pervasive influence of *The Rose Garden*.

In the case of these writers another interesting point deserves mention. In *Az Sabâ tâ Nimâ* [From Sabâ to Nimâ], Yahyâ Âryanpur lists twelve prominent, nineteenth-century prose writers, along with a sample from their works.[25] All of them are members of the court and in government service, except for one cleric named Mirza 'Abdollatif Tasuji. But even he is in the service of the court and responsible for the education of the crown prince Nâseroddin Mirza (1831–1896). Furthermore, his work in prose has no connection with religion, but is a famous translation of the Arabic *A Thousand and One Nights*. Not even a single name from among the ranks of Sufi mystics appears in the list.

From the end of the nineteenth, and the beginning of the twentieth century, i.e., from the period before the Constitution, both our prose and our social ethics find new paths, resulting in the birth, as it were, of a different practical philosophy.

---

23. Bahâr, *Study of Style*, vol. 3, p. 320.

24. [MH] Eqbâl, 'Abbâs, *Tarikh-e Mofassal-e Iran* . . . [Detailed History of Iran, vol 1: History of the Mongols] (Tehran: Amir Kabir, 1977, fourth printing). p. 541–3.

25. Yahyâ Âryânpur, *Az Sabâ tâ Nimâ* [From Sabâ to Nimâ], 2 vols. (Tehran: Ketâb-ha-ye Jibi, 1972).

The Muslim Clergy and Persian Prose

Muslim clerics [*ruhâniyân*] have usually been called *'olamâ* [learned, scholars; plural of *'âlem*] because they are people of science [*'elm*]. Their science is the science of religion. There is a Prophetic Tradition which says that science is twofold, the science of religion and the science of bodies, or theology and medicine. According to another Prophetic Tradition, Mohammad asserted that "the learned among my people are superior to the prophets of Israel." These *'olamâ* of the Muslim community are those very people who know the science of religion. Another Prophetic Tradition calls them the heirs to the prophets.[1]

---

1 [MH] For sources on *hadith*s [Prophetic Traditions], see Munawar Ahmad Anees and Alia N. Athar, *Guide to Sira and Hadith Literature in Western Languages* (New York, NY: Mansell Publishing Limited, 1986). A representative sampling of *hadith*s in English and Arabic appears in Maulana Mohammad Ali, *A Manual of Hadith*, preface by C.E. Bosworth (Atlantic Highlands, NJ: Humanities Press, Inc., 1978, first published in 1944).

Learning and the Language of Learning

When the term *'elm* [learning] was used in general and without qual-
ification, the science of religion was meant. When the term "scholar"
(*dâneshmand*) was used, religious jurisprudent [*faqih*] was intended. A
scholar who attains the level of exercise of judgment [*ejtehâd*] in Islamic
laws and edicts is a *mojtahed*, a scholar, period. Now if a person knows,
for example, astronomy, geography, alchemy, history, or arithmetic and
geometry, he is a scientist or scholar of astronomy, geometry, history,
alchemy and the like, but not a scholar or scientist in general, not like
someone expert in Islamic jurisprudence [*faqih*].

Moreover, in the view of the Muslim faithful, and especially the
religious scholars, the science of religion is not just a science, but
rather the only true science. Because it is divine science, the science
of prophets, and the source of salvation, it establishes the believer's
duty in this world and accounts for his salvation in the next. Other
things in human science are metaphorical and incomplete, subject
to error, and mostly a source of misguidance. They are useful and
worth learning only to the point where they are relevant to the
business of religion, for example, in determining the times of day
and night for prayer. Among Persian texts on this subject one can
refer to Hojviri's *Kashf al-Mahjûb* (c. 1060).[2] At the beginning of
the book, one of the first Sufi texts written in Persian, appears a
brief but adequate and clear exposition of the Muslim conception
of science and its aim, the usefulness of science leading to action
and the uselessness and detriment of science not leading to action.
On the same subject one might also cite a very famous and essential
Shi'i work, namely the Arabic *Kitâb al-Kâfi* [Book of Sufficiency]
by al-Kulaynî (d. 939), or *Ihyâ 'ulum al-din* [Vivification of Religious
Sciences] by Mohammad Ghazâli (d. 1111), the most famous work
of all. But here I shall quote briefly from *'Ayn al-hayât* [Wellspring
of Life] by Mohammad Bâqer Majlesi (1627–1698), the renowned
and powerful cleric and religious scholar of the later Safavid era.
In Majlesi's words: "It is reported of Imam Musa Kâzem that the
Prophet of God . . . declared that science is of these three sorts:
(1) clear divine signs of divine guidance in the Koran, or (2)
religious duty and necessity that He in His justice has ordained,

---

2. [MH] 'Ali b. 'Osmân Hojviri (d.c. 1072), *Kashf al-Mahjub* [Uncovering the Hid-
den]; translated by R.A. Nicholson as *The Kashf al-Mahjub, The Oldest Persian Treatise
on Sufism* (London: Luzac, 1959; Lahore, 1976; first printed in 1911),

or (3) Prophetic Traditions that remain in force until Resurrection Day. Anything other than these three is superfluous and without function."[3]

In the view of religious scholars, then, science is basically limited to the science of religion. That is to say, their own sciences, Islamic law, jurisprudence, Prophetic Traditions, Koranic commentaries, speculative theology, hagiography, and the rest; in accordance with Majlesi's classification, that which is related to the Koran, to Islamic law, and to Tradition. Where classifications of other religious scholars differ, they do so not in general or essential matters, but only in details.

In order to popularize this science among Muslims, that is, for them to execute their religious duties, the religious scholars of Islam dealt with two classes and in general employed two methods: first, with other religious scholars, i.e., their own class, people of learning and science; and second, with the mass of illiterate or only slightly literate believers. The vehicle they utilized in the scholarly communication among themselves was the Arabic language; and their method of communication was writing. They wrote on the science of religion in Arabic for persons acquainted with science, because religion was science, and the language of science in Islamic civilization in all Muslim countries was Arabic, much like (as has often been noted, but let me also repeat it) Latin in medieval Europe. They wrote in Arabic not only about theology and Prophetic Traditions, but also about astronomy or, for example, medicine. Moreover, the language of religion (aside from the fact of the "scientific" nature of religion) was likewise Arabic: God's words in the Koran and the Prophet's words in Traditions. The language of the Prophet's family and his friends and of the government of Islam was Arabic. Arabic was a sacred language. Meanings, idioms and expressions, and the growth and expansion of religion, took place and achieved results in the Arabic words of the Arabs. Although in the eleventh century Persian found its way into the sanctuary of religion through translation of the Koran, Arabic remained the language of religion for two reasons. One was that it was the language of science, and science was in Arabic. Second was the fact that it was the language of revelation and had a sacred character. Experts in science of any sort

---

3. Mohammad Bâqer b. Mohammad Taqi Majlesi, *'Ayn al-hayât dar vasâyâ-ye hazrat-e rasul* [Wellspring of Life on the Counsels of the Prophet], edited by 'Ali Akbar al-Ghaffâri (Tehran, 1970). [MH] On Majlesi, see Abdul-Hadi Hairi, "Madjlisî," *Encyclopaedia of Islam (New Edition)* 5 (1985): 1086–1088.

were obliged to know this language, which they did, and by means of which they established communication with one another. In addition, because of the evolutionary preparedness and capacity of the language, the exposition of scientific points in Arabic was particularly precise and expressive and prevailed throughout the Islamic empire.

As explained earlier, writing in Persian was bound up, especially at the beginning, with a sense of nationality, as we saw in the case of civil administrators and officials. But such a motive did not exist for writing Persian on the part of religious scholars. Islam is a religion which is theoretically alien to ethnic group identity, nationality, or racial pride—in contrast, for example, with the Zoroastrian faith, which was exclusively Iranian, or Judaism, which declared the children of Israel to be the chosen people of Yahweh, the God of one people. Islam declared the faithful to be brothers. The principle was faith, and what differentiated one was belief or unbelief, not whether one was Arab or Persian or Turkish or Tajik. Of course, Muslims vied with one another in terms of ethnic origin. Everyone knows the stories about the Umayyad Caliphs (ruled 661–750) and the *mawâli* [non-Arab Muslims]. But this rivalry was not based on Islamic religious approval, but rather on realities stemming from the fabric and culture of Islamic societies. In short, the point is that for a self-conscious believer, and all the more for the religious scholar, being Iranian or not did not matter. What was important was being a Muslim or not.

Mohammad Ghazâli, author of *Vivification of Religious Sciences* and one of Islam's most esteemed scholars, was born approximately fifty years after the death of Ferdowsi and in the same city of Tus. But it is hard to believe that he was from Ferdowsi's city. Of Ghazâli, Jalâloddin Homâ'i says: "His national feelings and ethnic sentiments and social customs and manners are transient and absorbed into the religious law and faith which he embraced. He sees everything in the mirror of religious rules, orders and duties. He considers everything which is beyond the pale of heavenly religious law to be ephemeral, vain and obnoxious."[4] It is for this reason that Ghazâli says: "Nowruz and *Sadeh* should be abolished and never mentioned . . . Things sold for Sadeh and Nowruz, such as shields, wooden swords and pottery trumpets, are not per se forbidden, but are forbidden as an expression of Zoro-

---

4. Jalâloddin Homâ'i, in the preface to his edition of Gunzali's *Nasihat al-moluk* [Advice to Kings] (Tehran, 1972), p. 77.

astrian slogans and are contrary to religious law. Whatever is done for such occasions is inappropriate."[5]

As will be shown below, epics and national legends, customs, and rites are "Zoroastrian" and "Magian" in the view of religious scholars. Consequently national feeling could not incite them to write in the national language (Persian). Even if they occasionally wrote something in this language, another motive was at work. They maintained links indirectly, by means of Arabic, with their own class, those expert in science. But because the primary religious and secular duty of religious scholars concerned the mass of believers and followers, scholars naturally made contact with them by means of the mother tongue, Persian. However, they did not do this in writing, but rather orally.

Oral Culture

In the past, when literacy was not widespread and science and literary culture were at the disposal of the elite alone, written cultural commentaries and transactions were likewise exclusively theirs, and not the property of everyone or even a majority. The transmission of culture among members of society took place over time and from one generation to the next mostly through oral means, such as tales told by old women, sermons in the name of the caliphs and sultans, rural love quatrains or stories told by professional raconteurs. In the realm of literacy, the method was constant repetition, formulaics and the recitation of religious anthems and chants, prayers, litanies, rote prayers, repetitions which encapsulate the essence of ethical teachings, cosmology, and the divine meanings of myths and sacraments (for example, the prayers or characterizations of the gods and demons that appear in the Avestan *Gatha*s and *Yasna*s and *Yasht*s again and again in the same form without variation so that, among other reasons, they might easily and correctly be committed to memory). These are the highest documents of oral culture wherein knowledge was transmitted from heart to heart and crafts from hand to hand, from master to apprentice. Owing to the sacred nature of these documents, they were not to be altered, but were to remain fixed and unchanging, like rock inscriptions.

---

5. Ibid., p. 78.

One of the principal occasions of poetry and metered and rhymed speech and poetry in religious literary culture was this very ease of memorization, which led to the spread of verse to other kinds of knowledge, such as medicine, astronomy, and language learning. In the arena of education, oral methods and oral views of cultural transmission had fundamental validity. For example, the "literate" person was one who had committed more things to memory. He was thought to be more learned and was held in greater esteem than someone with a deeper, broader and more methodical power of thought, but who had committed less knowledge to memory. It was said of poets that they first memorized several thousand couplets of verse and then claimed to be poets. By this means their art or profession became second nature to them. Many examples could be given, but the point is obvious: the unquestioned importance of oral methods in the transmission of culture.

The religious scholar, too, utilized this oral method for establishing contact with ordinary people and transmitting knowledge of religion among the faithful. And he had all of the oral means at his disposal, from the mosque, seminary, *tekyeh* (dervish retreat), the streets and the bazaar to pilgrimage sites and private homes, while traveling and at home and at every other place imaginable. Here religious scholars and other clerics, in these places, depending upon the occasion, preached sermons formal and informal, and discussed religious issues. From the pulpit, they expatriated on the tragedy of Karbala, on other Shi'i martyrs, and delivered elegies and eulogies. More important than all of this is the fact that in villages and cities, owing to practical needs and problems of living, they had constant and daily contact with Muslims. All of this made writing unnecessary in their communication.

In this fashion, writing in Persian held no special attraction for religious scholars, who wrote about religious science among themselves in Arabic, had oral communication with the faithful, and were not encouraged to write by any national feeling. They wrote less in Persian in comparison with government officials and Sufis, at least up to the Safavid period.

Now, Persian translations of the Koran and Koranic commentaries are another matter altogether. From the very beginning religious scholars were involved in the writing of Persian in these areas of their expertise. Extant commentaries, which, by the way, are a great treasure of the Persian language and vocabulary, are evidence of this involvement. Examples, some of them outstanding works of Persian prose, are: *Tafsir-e kabir* [The Great Commentary], *Tafsir-e Qor'ân-e Pâk* [The Commentary on the Pure Koran], the so-called *Cambridge Commentary*, the commentary of Abu Bakr 'Atiq Surâbâdi[6] and Maybodi's *Kashf al-asrâr* [Disclosure of Secrets]. But this branch of religious scholarship aside, in other areas the works of religious scholars in the national language are no more than a handful in the first centuries of the appearance and spread of Persian prose. One of the first surviving pieces of Persian prose is the already-cited tenth-century treatise on Hanafi theology by Abolqâsem Samarqandi (d. 953). The treatise called *Kefâyeh* [Adequacy] by Imam al-Boghavi al-Shafe'i and an expository treatise on principles of Sunni belief by Mohammad b. Ahmad Nasafi (d. 1310) can also be mentioned. Later, in the fourteenth century, several other works in various branches of religious science are written in Persian, among them *Bayân al-Adyân* [Explanation of Religion] by Abu al-Ma'âli 'Alavi Râzi, and *Tabserat al-'avâm va ma'refat al-mazâheb* [Advice to the People and Knowledge of Religious Sects]. But, as asserted above, such works are very limited in number, especially in comparison with major works by court and Sufi writers.

In short, in the periods when Persian prose achieved official status and later spread throughout Iran and a great number of its most important works were written, religious scholars, both Sunni and Shi'i, did not have a significant role in these developments.

The Isma'ilis and the Persian Language

Because the Isma'ilis enjoyed a special situation in the very context under discussion, a few words need to be said about them before proceeding to the Twelver Shi'is. Isma'ili writers and thinkers began to use Persian in writings on religious matters before religious scholars of other Muslim sects and groups. Besides such famous works of Nâser Khosrow (c. 1004–c. 1088) as *Jâme' al-hekmatayn* [Philosophical Compendium], *Zâd al-mosâferin* [Provisions for Travelers] and *Vajh-e din* [Substance of Religion], one can cite as examples Sejestâni's *Kashf al-Mahjub* [Revelation of the Hidden] or *Sharh-e Qasideh-ye Abu'l-Haysam* [Exposition of Abu al-Haytham's Qasideh] by Mohammad b.

---

6. [MH] Abu Bakr 'Atiq Surâbâdi, *Tafsir-e Qor'ân-e Karim* [Commentary on the Noble Koran] (Tehran, 1967).

Sorkh Neyshâbur.[7] According to Safa in *History of Literature in Iran*, "Some historians and other writers accused the sects of the Isma'ilis, Carmathians and others of apostasy from Islam and of pretending to be Muslim for the dual purpose of destroying Islam and of renewing Magian customs. If this indictment is correct, the appearance of Isma'ilism in Iran was accompanied by national aims and goals. Al-Baghdâdi gives numerous pieces of evidence in support of this view and has dated the beginning of the activity of this group from the time of the caliph Mo'tasem when Bâbak and Mâzyâr had revolted with the aim of renewing ancient beliefs and customs."[8] After summarizing such evidence as their dualism, reverence for fire, belief in placing a fire container in every mosque, and interpretation of Islamic rules in a fashion compatible with Zoroastrianism, Safa reaches this conclusion: "Because of this nationalist aim, the Isma'ili call attracted many followers in Iran during the tenth and eleventh centuries, when a great number of prominent and famous men were exposed to this religion. Among them, Nasr b. Ahmad the Samanid and many leading men of Bokhara converted to Isma'ilism."[9]

Among religious people, those Isma'ilis whose works were in Persian were situated differently from other Muslims with respect to politics. They were Shi'i, and opposed to Sunni sects and the Baghdad caliphate. In addition, they possessed the largest "political-ideological" organization opposed to the government and the religion of the government, not only in this period but perhaps throughout the Islamic history of Iran. The point here is not the "political-ideological" beliefs of the Isma'ili organization or the methods of their social activism. But with its already cited characteristics, the movement possessed a culture and cultural approach peculiar to itself. As is well

7. [MH] E.g., Naser-e Khosrow, *Vajh-e din* [Substance of Religion], edited by Gholamrezâ Aavani, with an English preface by Sayyid Hossein Nasr (Tehran: Iranian Academy of Philosophy, 1977). Another of Nâser-e Khosrow's prose works available in English is *Safarnâma: Nâser Khosraw's Book of Travels*, translated by W.M. Thackston (Albany, NY: SUNY Press, 1986). From his poetry, there is *Forty Poems from the Divan of Nasir-i Khusraw*, translated by Peter Lamborn Wilson and Gholâmrezâ Aavani (Tehran: Iranian Academy of Philosophy, 1977).

8. Vol. 1, p. 252. One can also refer to A.E. Bertels, *Nâser Khosrow va Esmâ'iliyân* [Nâser Khosrow and the Isma'ilis], translated by Âryânpur (Tehran: Bonyâd-e Farhang-e Iran, 1967), pp. 60 ff., where Muslim histories are cited in regard to the Isma'ilis Zoroastrian leanings and their enmity toward Islam.

9. *History of Literature in Iran*, vol. 1, p. 253.

known, from the time of Nâser Khosrow and Hasan Sabbâh, and before and after them, the Isma'ilis engaged wholeheartedly in propaganda and conversion, in gathering more followers and organizing them for the purpose of religio-political struggle. But on the path to the achievement of their ends, they had at their disposal scarcely any of the oral vehicles that the Sunni establishment had. Therefore, they naturally chose other vehicles—written means, writing itself.

Another important point is the religious and political opposition of the Isma'ilis to the Baghdad caliphate. They accepted neither the spiritual nor the temporal rule of the Caliphate. This opposition was firm, intense and mostly bloody on both sides. Thus, although the Isma'ilis were Muslims, they did not have as strong an attachment to the language of the Baghdad caliphate (Arabic) as did the religious scholars of other Muslim sects and schools. In their view, the caliphate belonged by right to the family of the Prophet and the Fatimids of Egypt, whose ancestry went back to the imams. But this "religio-political" belief did not greatly affect the Persian writing of the Isma'ilis and their language, both because connections between the center of the Fâtemid caliphate in Cairo and the center of the Persian language and Isma'ili activity in Khorâsân were loose, mediated and mostly theoretical, and because other geographical and political barriers existed. As a result, the cultural influence of the Fâtemid center on the Isma'ilis of Iran, particularly with respect to language, was not strong and did not lead them toward a use of Arabic.

The Isma'ilis of Iran confronted as enemies the Baghdad caliphate, the regional Iranian governments (which were Sunni and cooperated with the caliphate) and the four Sunni schools of theology and their scholars. In the struggle against these strong enemies, the Isma'ilis relied chiefly on local people, the people of Iran who all, even if they did not speak Persian in a given locale, still used Persian as their official and written language. Because they had to derive their total strength from this people, the Isma'ilis soon adopted their language. Among all of the Muslim religious sects scattered throughout Iran, they were the only group that wrote mostly in Persian rather than Arabic. And for the business of religion and politics, which in their view were inseparable, they paid more attention to the local language than to the language of religion. In that period, in cultural and political terms and in thought and deed, the Isma'ilis played a national role, in which regard this religio-political movement had a significant share in the evolution and spread of Persian prose. In Safa's words:

> The Isma'ilis are very important in Persian literary culture, specifically in their intense interest in writing numerous books and articles in the Persian language. Because the sect's basis for success lay in proselytizing and conversion, they perforce disseminated their aims through the language of the people of the region.
> Consequently, they attached great importance to writing books and treatises and composing verse in Persian. We have treatises, books, and verse by Isma'ili propagandists and leaders from the tenth century onward. The most prominent Isma'ili poet and writer is Nâser Khosrow, who was active in proselytizing and writing both prose and poetry in the second half of the eleventh century . . . Numerous other writers in the various Isma'ili fortresses were busy during this whole period writing books in Persian. Nearly all of them were eventually removed from libraries and burned in the course of conflicts and the conquest of Isma'ili strongholds. The authorship of books, treatises and poems supporting Isma'ili views resulted in that sect's great influence on Persian literature, an influence which continually draws our attention to the sect in our research on Persian literary works before the Mongol invasion."[10]

Periodization of Twelver Shiism

On the subject of the history of Shiism, there are differing views resulting in different periodizations, which depend mostly on how Shi'i jurisprudence was codified, or on the question of the imamate and other purely religious considerations. The periodization presented by Henri Corbin in *En Islam Iranien* is a good illustration of such chronologies. Corbin divides the history of Twelver Shiism into these four periods: (1) from the beginning to the major occultation of the Hidden Imam in 873; (2) from the disappearance of the Twelfth Imam to Nâsiroddin Tusi (1200–1274); (3) from Tusi's death to the rise of the Safavids in 1501; and (4) from the Safavids (1501–1736) to the Qâjârs (1796–1925) and today.[11] The logic of this periodization is clear. In the first period (632–873) the Twelve Imams are present and serve in religious issues of theology, Prophetic Traditions, and the rest as models of Shi'i behavior and the source of solutions to their difficulties. In the

---

10. *History of Literature in Iran*, vol. 2, p. 179.
11. [MH] Henri Corbin (1898–1977), *En Islam Iranien* [In Iranian Islam] (Paris: Gallimard, 1971).

second period (873–1274), when such living sources of emulation are no longer on the scene, Shi'i religious sciences are developed, among them jurisprudence, the recording of Prophetic Traditions, and Koranic commentaries. The third period (1274–1501) is a continuation of the second in terms of the evolution of the religious sciences, and concludes with the achievement of official status by the Shi'i in Iran. In the fourth period (1501–1925 and beyond), with the Isfahan School and such outstanding representatives as Mir Dâmâd (c. 1561–1630) and Mollâ Sadrâ (1571–1640), Shi'i thought continues on the path of expansion and evolution. Despite such figures as Majlesi and the Usuli religious scholars of the Zand Era and the beginning of the Qajar Period, the sciences of Prophetic Traditions, theology, jurisprudence and religious law in general are brought to completion.

But for our purposes in appreciating the role of Shi'i religious scholars in the evolution of Persian prose, periodizations such as Corbin's are inadequate. Because we must focus on social dimensions of the religion and its political and cultural effects, the history of Shiism might be better divided into the following five periods, each exhibiting a distinctive social and political character: (1) from the beginning to the rise of the Safavid state, 632–1501; (2) the Safavid era, 1501–1736; (3) from the fall of the Safavids to the beginning of the Constitutional Movement, 1736–1906; (4) the Constitutional era, 1906–1911; (5) the Pahlavi era, from the coup d'état in 1921 to the Islamic Revolution of 1978 and 1979.

In the first period, Shiism is without governmental power. Although it achieved it for a time through such dynasties as the Buyids and Sarbedârs, it was still not the religion of the majority, of which the Baghdad caliphate was the official representative. In the second period, Shiism has governmental power, political and cultural control, and is the religion of the majority, a special relation existing between religion and state. The third period, except for the brief reign of Nader Shah Afshâr (ruled 1736–1747), is a period of weakened central government, power on the part of religious scholars, and the perfection of the "socio-religious" structure of Shiism. In the fourth period, Twelver Shiism struggles against non-religious government, represented by Qajar dictatorship (1796–1925) and colonialist modernism, which comes from the West and is imported chiefly by the English and the Russians. On the subject of the fifth and final period, because it is still in progress and concerns our present, one must either say nothing or speak at great length. Just as in the case of the political role of Shiism or its religious scholars in the Constitutional Movement, where my view is not in accord with general and received opinion, to pass on with no more than a brief discussion would likely create only ambiguities.

The Political and Cultural Role of Shiism in the First Period (632–1501)

Let us then return to the first period (632–1501) and the political and cultural role of Shiism in our Islamic history up to the rise of the Safavids with respect to nationality and language. Concerning an issue of this magnitude, which has loud echoes in every period of history, or a living and active religious phenomenon with continuous effects on the course of events, both active and passive in its involvement with events and historical currents, and with various, sometimes even contradictory, social features and dimensions, generalizations can be useless and misleading. This danger notwithstanding, there must be some place for discussion of generalities.

During the first centuries of the Islamic era, when the national feeling of Iranians after the Arab Muslim conquest was gradually taking shape and being realized, such groups, sects and organizations as the Khorramdins and the supporters of Ibn al-Moqanna' fought not only against Arab domination but also with Islam. Besides them, some Muslim Iranians were likewise not happy with the government of the Arabs because, especially from the Umayyads (661–750) onward, Arab government in the name of Islam was marked by pillage, plunder, bloodletting, and self-glorification. In a word, things were oppressive. We know that Abu Muslim and the people of Khorâsân were the essential factor in the collapse of the Umayyads and the transfer of the caliphate to the 'Abbâsids (750–1258). According to I.P. Petrushevskii (1898–1977) in *Islam in Iran*, in Abu Muslim's rebellion which began at Marv in Khorâsân on 25 Ramazan 747, "Shiites, Kharijites from Sistan, and the Zoroastrian sect of Khorramites took part."[12] Some seventy years later, in 813 C.E., the 'Abbâsid caliph Ma'mun, relying on these same Khorâsân troops, was able to wrest the caliphate and its capital, Baghdad, from his brother Amin. Ma'mun's vizier Fazl-e Sahl was a Shi'i, and the fact that to attract support from the people of Khorâsân the caliph designated the eighth

---

12. I.P. Petrushevskii, *Eslâm dar Iran* [Islam in Iran], translated by Karim Keshâvarz (Tehran: Enteshârât-e Payâm, 1975), p. 69.

Shi'i Imam as his successor and invited him to Khorâsân shows the
extent of Shi'i influence and power. But in his army there were not
only Shiites, but all manner of Muslims. The commander-in-chief
Tâher Zu'l-yaminayn was, like Ma'mun, a member of the Sunni sect.
On the subject of these Shi'i and Sunni aides of the caliph, the historian Abolfazl Bayhaqi writes:

> When Amin was killed and the caliphate reached Ma'mun, he
> remained for more than two years in Marv. And that is a long story.
> The vizier Fazl-e Sahl wanted the caliphate taken from the
> 'Abbâsids and given to the 'Alids. He reminded Ma'mun that the
> latter had made a vow on his grave and had sworn that if Almighty
> God put and end to his brother's rule and he became caliph, he
> would name an 'Alid as his heir. Fazl-e Sahl reminded him that he
> had not kept his oath and vow. Ma'mun responded by admitting the
> truth of what Fazl-e Sahl said and by asking who should be named
> his successor. Fazl-e Sahl said: 'Ali b. Musa al-Reza who is the Imam
> of the age and who resides in the city of the Prophet.' Ma'mun said:
> "Someone has to be sent secretly to inform Tâher in writing to the
> effect that this and that will be done so that we will send someone
> to bring 'Ali b. Musa al-Reza from Medina for people to swear
> allegiance to in secret and that he be sent by a good route to Marv
> so that here the oath of allegiance and his succession be made
> known."

Fazl-e makes preparations for the enterprise and gives the news to
Tâher. As for Ma'mun's general, according to Bayhaqi:

> This news pleased Tâher because he had an inclination to the
> 'Alids. He arranged things as charged, and he named a trustworthy
> man from his own staff to accompany Ma'mun's trustworthy
> representative. The two of them proceeded to Medina, spoke to
> Reza in private, presented him with the letter, and gave him the
> messages. Reza was averse to the proposal because he knew that
> things would not work out, but he acceded because there was no
> way out of Ma'mun's command. So he came surreptitiously and in
> disguise to Baghdad, where they housed him in a good place. After
> he had rested for a week, Tâher visited him at night very secretively,
> and treated him with great respect. He presented to him the letter
> in Ma'mun's handwriting and said: "I am the first who will swear
> allegiance to you at the command of my lord, the prince of the

faithful; and once I have sworn allegiance, there are 1,000 cavalry and foot-soldiers with me who will all swear allegiance."[13]

The remainder of the story is not relevant to our discussion. Instead, let us look briefly at the Barmakis and the issue of the 'Alids a little before this. During the caliphate of Ma'mun's father Hârun al-Rashid (ruled 786–809), one of the 'Alids in Gorgân and Tabarestân rebelled and attracted a following. The caliph, after consultation with his vizier Yahyâ b. Khâled Barmaki, sent the latter's son Fazl Barmaki to quell the insurrection and gave him the provinces of Khorâsân, Rayy, Jebâl, Khârazm, Sistan, and Transoxiana to govern. According to Bayhaqi, before Fazl's departure, his father said to him:

> Son, this is a major enterprise that the Caliph has charged you with and a high rank in this world that he has conferred upon you. But in the next world, there will be a severe punishment, for you must overthrow one of the Prophet's progeny, peace be upon him. Other than obedience there is no course, for we have many enemies and are suspected of being partisans of the 'Alids." Fazl said: "Do not be concerned, I shall persevere, even if it costs me my life in settling this matter fully.[14]

These several examples demonstrate that many Iranians were not sympathetic to the Umayyad and 'Abbâsid caliphal courts and were attracted to their rivals not only for religious, but also for social, political, and cultural reasons, and in general out of nationalist motives.

This attitude of Iranian Shiites, that the caliphate belonged to the family of the Prophet and that other caliphs were usurpers, was naturally deeper and broader than that. Let us look at the issue from another vantage point, psychological and emotional: the marriage of Imam Hosayn to an Iranian princess. It is said that the fourth Imam is the son of this woman, which is to say that Iranian blood runs in the race of the imams. Doubtful historical accuracy notwithstanding, the psychological effect of the fact of the historical rumor among Iranian Shiites is certain. Just as, on the other side of this coin, only God knows to what extent the tales told about the caliph Omar are true or not. Nevertheless the antipathy toward Omar, during whose caliphate Iran was conquered, is a fact and has apparently existed from early on. For example, it is a fact that Omar's assassin was Iranian. In any case,

---

13. Bayhaqi's *History*, p. 141.
14. Ibid., p. 415.

besides religious and social reasons, Shiites also felt themselves emotionally related in a special way to the family of the prophet and the imamate and consequently alien to the Baghdad caliphate.

The Political and Cultural Role of the Buyids

Discussion of the political and cultural role of Shiism in the first period is not possible without discussion of the Buyid Dynasty (945–1055). We know that they were of the people of Daylam, in the western Alborz. In the tenth and eleventh centuries they ruled over Fârs, Jebâl, Azerbaijan, Khuzistan and Iraq. At that period, the Sasanians controlled the northern and northeastern regions of the Iranian plateau, and the Buyids the central, southern and western regions as far as Iraq. Zaydi Shiites, the Buyids later converted to Twelver Shiism.[15] But they had a religious policy untinged with fanaticism and simplistic views. In administrative matters they pursued practical realities for the most part, rather than the implementation of their religious convictions. After they extended their power from the north into the Iranian plateau, they became aware of Baghdad. By the year 932 they had achieved control over the major portion of the Iranian plateau. In 945, they gained Baghdad.

Now let us take note of a few, telling historical realities which help characterize this period. The Buyids were Iranian and Shi'i. After the conquest of Baghdad, they ruled over the main part of the caliphal lands. The religion of the majority of people over whom the Buyids ruled was Sunni Islam. In Rayy, Hamadân and Isfahan, despite their high government positions, Buyid leaders remained Zoroastrian.[16] The language of the Daylamites was of the Iranian family of languages, but was not Persian, although their leaders spoke Persian.

In light of these historical realities, the Buyids opposed the Baghdad caliphate in terms of group identity, religion, and, more important, political rivalry, and they achieved control over that caliphate. Ahmad, the son of Buyeh, entered Baghdad in 945 and obtained the title "Mu'izz al-dawla" from the caliphal Mustakfi. Eleven days later

---

15.　See *The Cambridge History of Iran*, vol. 4 (1975), p. 256. [MH] On the Buyids, see also Claude Cahen, "Buwayhids or Buyids," *Encyclopaedia of Islam* (New Edition) 1 (1960): 1350–1357.

16.　Ahmad Bahmanyâr, *Sharh-e hâl-e Sâheb ebn-e 'Abbâd* [The Life of the Sâhib Ibn 'Abbâd] (Tehran: Enteshârât-e Dâneshgâh-e Tehran, 1955), p. 103.

Ahmad removed al-Mustakfi and "summoned Abu'l-qâsem Fazl b. Muqtadir to the caliphal palace and named him caliph, swore allegiance to him and gave him the title 'al-Muti' li-llâh' [Obedient to God].[17] The Baghdad caliphs were to remain powerless under Buyid control for a period of 109 years, while Buyid princes ruled. Mu'izz al-dawla intended to remove the Sunni caliph, procure allegiance for one of the leaders of the 'Alid family, and thus replace a Sunni with a Shi'i caliph. But he later changed his mind, apparently for various reasons. One was the existence of a Sunni majority among Muslims in both Iran and Iraq, in the "interior" and "foreign" lands of the Buyids. Because Sunnis believed in the legitimacy of the 'Abbâsid caliphate, its overthrow was likely to create serious political and sectarian problems. Second was the fact that the Buyid army in general was composed of two groups: Shi'i Daylamites and Gilânis, and Sunni Turks and Kurds. The Buyids endeavored to maintain a balance among them. In addition, coming to terms with a weak and obedient caliph was preferable to serving a caliph whose legitimacy they themselves recognized and to whose will they would have to accede when a dispute arose.

Consequently, the Shi'i king and the Sunni caliph remained. An accommodation prevailed between monarchy and caliphate, between Shiism and Sunnism, between Iranian and Arab, and between worldly and religious power. Both sides accepted a sort of symbiosis which was in their best interests. Pursuant to this very policy, 'Azud al-dawla later married his own daughter to the caliph. The Hâshemite caliph bestowed title, robes of honor, and legitimacy to 'Azud al-dawla, who considered himself the successor to the Sasanian emperors. In exchange, at the Friday congregational prayer the sermon was offered in the name of a caliph who no longer had political and military power. The government operated in his name and on his behalf, and the Shiites, in contrast with their past behavior, attended the Friday prayer.

After the conquest of Baghdad, the Buyids played both sides against the middle. Under the banner of the caliph, their government over Sunni subjects found legitimacy, especially in Iraq; and they pursued their own sectarian activities. In the year 325 A.H. (= 936 C.E.) Mu'izz al-dawla ordered shops closed in Baghdad on 'Âshurâ and mourning to be observed. On 'Ayd-e Ghadir in the same year he ordered decora-

17. 'Ali Asghar Faqihi, *Âl-e Buyeh va Owzâ'-e Zamân-e Ishân* [The Buyids and Conditions during Their Age] (Tehran: Enteshârât-e Sabâ, 1978), p. 141.

tions and celebrations throughout the city. In the Buyid period, jurisprudence, theology, traditions and Shi'i "science of religion" in general ripened to maturity and bore fruit. The sunset of Kulayni coincided with the dawn of the Buyids. Sayyid Razi, compiler of the *Nahj al-balâgha* [The Manner of Eloquence], Shaykh Mofid, Shaykh Tusi, and Sayyid Mortaza, all of whom were among the leading Shi'i religious scholars, all lived in this era and in Baghdad. Ibn Babuyeh had meetings of discussion with the Buyid prince Ruka al-dawla and was accorded the latter's respect,[18] and Sayyid Razi had a similar relationship with Bahâ al-dawla.

As for Buyid nationality, because they were aware of their national identity and Iranianness, they consequently in a sense had a national policy. As already stated, the sons of Buyeh the fisherman traced their ancestry back to the Sasanians. In accordance with pre-Islamic Iranian custom, 'Azud al-dawla had given himself the title of *shâhanshâh* [emperor]. The capture of Baghdad itself, which had become the successor capital to Sasanian Ctesiphon, realized an old national desire which princes such as Ya'qub nurtured. The Ziyârid Mardâvij was the last prince immediately before the Buyids to express this desire. He also considered himself *shâhanshâh*, revitalized ancient customs, and wanted to overturn the caliph and rule imperially as the Sasanians had done. It so happens that the brothers Buyeh before achieving independence were commanders for Mâkân Kâki and this very Mardâvij. All of them were new converts to Islam (or, like Mardâvij, non-Muslim), all from the people of northern Iran, neighbors geographically and relatives anthropologically.

Not only princes and kings but also a prominent vizier like the Sahib ibn 'Abbâd, who displayed fanaticism in religion and language (Arabic), did not consider his race lowly. In Ahmad Bahmanyâr's words, "if such was the case, he never mentioned his origins and language in his own verse and prose and his poets as well in abiding by his practice did not allude to this subject in their poetry either . . . the Sâhib's poets mentioned his Sasanian lineage with respect in their poetry."[19]

The Buyids captured Baghdad but, as stated above, kept the caliph and administered their empire from the caliphal residence in his name in governing the Sunnis and despite him in governing the Shi'is. That

18. Ibid., p. 278.
19. Bahmanyâr, *Life of the Sahib*, p. 104.

ancient desire had been achieved with awareness of practical and political considerations and the limitations that necessarily obtain in the
exercise of authority.

> Although 'Adud al-Dawla did not return to Shiraz again, it continued
> to be regarded as the actual capital of the empire, and it was from
> Fârs that were drawn the civil servants who replaced most of 'Izz
> al-Daela's civil service in Baghdad . . . The supreme judge in
> Baghdad was also dismissed and exiled, and his successor now resided
> in Shiraz and was represented in Baghdad by four deputy judges, a
> decision which infringed the traditional rights of the caliph severely
> and which also provides an eloquent illustration of the shift of
> balance from Baghdad to Shiraz. . . . The main offices of state
> continued to be located in Shiraz.[20]

Whereas 'Azud al-dawla himself resided in Baghdad for political
reasons.

But despite these symptoms which bespeak both attention to group
identity and the political ambitions of Buyid leaders, their policies were
not "national" in the limited sense of the word, as a policy designed
for and limited to one nation. One reason may have been that their
empire was "international." They became established in Baghdad, the
center of a part of the world of Islam. In the north and south of Iraq
and elsewhere, they ruled over peoples who were neither Iranian nor
Persian-speaking. For that matter in parts of their Iran, for example
in Azerbaijan or Khuzistan, neither the Persian language nor national
feeling had taken root and grown limbs and sprouted leaves as with
the people of Khorâsân. Because of their proximity to Iraq and the
Baghdad court, Khuzistan, Jebâl, the west and parts of central Iran
were more influenced by the culture and rule of the Arabs than were
such distant regions as Sistan and Transoxiana. Moreover, in the
Iranian lands of the Buyids, local languages and dialects prevailed: in
Azerbaijan, Khuzistan, Daylam, Tabarestân and Gilan, Âzari, Khuzi,
Daylami, Tabari, and Gili, respectively, were spoken, while Kurdish
was spoken in Kurdestan. In Jebâl they apparently still spoke Middle
Persian (Pahlavi).

From one "Bandar-e Râzi" and several of his surviving poems we
know that in the tenth century the people of Rayy not only had a
special dialect, but also composed poetry in it, just as several couplets

---

20. *The Cambridge History of Iran*, vol. 4, p. 271.

from Sa'di and Hafez show that for centuries after that the inhabitants of 'Azud al-dawla's capital, Shiraz, spoke in their own dialect. The eleventh-century poet Qatrân "was the first person to compose Persian poetry in Azerbaijan."[21] In most of these regions Persian [*fârsi-ye dari*] was understood and was in general use, but not with the pervasive vitality it had in Khorâsân and Transoxiana, where such local languages as Sogdian, Tocharian, and Khwarezmian had less vitality and could not survive the onslaught of Persian.

The Buyid Empire comprised several nationalities, religions, and languages. It was not like the government of the Sasanians, which was local, with, selectively, a single language and one religious sect, belonging to one people. Perhaps for this reason the Buyid policy toward language also was different from that of the Sasanians. Instead of Persian, the Buyids favored Arabic, the "international language" of the Islamic lands. Although such prominent viziers as Ibn-e 'Amid and the Sâhib ibn 'Abbâd were Iranian, they were literary personalities in Arabic. Abu'l-Faraj al-Isfahani and Ibn al-Nadim, the authors of *Kitâls al-Aghâni* [The Bode of Songs] and *al-Fihrist* [The Catalogue] respectively, or Ibn Miskuwayh, the famous historian and literary figure, operated in the Buyid system and under their patronage. All three were important writers in Arabic.

This discussion of the Buyids here draws to a close with a comparison between them and the Sasanians, both of whom were more or less in the same historical period, were political rivals, and together ruled over the whole of Iran. The Sasanians were Sunnis, the religion of the Baghdad caliphate, and were in accord with the caliphate in the matter of government. Their national policy was self-conscious and firmly grounded in a foundation of language and history. The Buyids were Shiites, and in conflict with the Baghdad caliphate (until they gained control over it). Their national policy was based on the twin foundations of religion and history. The difference was that for the Sasanians history gave reality to a national identity, whereas for the Buyids it was a matter of the background and identity of a family (the Buyids) and its political-national aims. Also, their Sunni faith was not influential in Sasanian national policy, whereas Shiism was influential with the Buyids and constituted a cornerstone of their politics vis-à-vis the Baghdad caliphate.

---

21. Safa, *History of Literature in Iran*, vol. 2, p. 423.

The Dichotomous Situation of Shiism in Culture and Politics

The Buyids were independent of the Baghdad caliphate (the government of the Arabs) in the political realm, but remained under Arab cultural domination in the realm of culture (language and literature). Their situation epitomizes the role that Shiism played generally during its first period. The Shi'i individual was in a continual state of separation or alienation from the Baghdad caliphate in terms of belief and sentiment. A sort of centrifugal force continually held him far from the caliphate of 'Abbâsid usurpers. By dint of his spurning Baghdad, he looked back to Rayy, Nishâbur, Herat, or any other place. Because of his religion he would fall politically into a "national" or at least native situation or locale. But because for a believer the principle in everything is religion, and nothing else, the force of faith would simultaneously and continually separate him from nationality. For this reason the Shiite was in a dichotomous situation.

In comparison with the Zaydis and the Isma'ilis, the Twelver Shi'i took shape later and exhibited a more moderate approach to political and religious struggles. For this reason as well, the Baghdad caliphate, the Iranian government and the Sunni community tolerated them. In general, Sunnis and Twelver Shi'is lived side by side as members of the same faith. At any rate, when political and military power was in the hands of the Twelver Shi'is (the Buyids), they played both ends against the middle as asserted earlier. But when they did not wield governmental power and were in the minority (in most places and from the era of the Sasanians to just before the Safavids), they exhibited a twofold behavior toward the dominant religion and government. The Shi'i stance toward the Sunni governmental system was that of seeking legal rights, being accepted like others in the society of Muslims, and having the right to live. When necessary, the Shi'i would dissemble; when his life was in danger he could conceal or deny his religion, and cast his lot with the government of the Sunnis. But the Shi'i's other face was his regard for his own beliefs not only that he might put them into practice but also that he might declare and promote them at every appropriate opportunity. Let us pass over the fact that this twofold behavior became responsible also for a two-faced personality and social ethics.

Let us return to the ambivalent situation of the Shiite in the face of the matter of nationality: both falling into the "nationalist" condition and fleeing it. This sense of nationhood, as observed earlier, was reactive and lacking in self-awareness. In self-awareness and insofar as beliefs are concerned, the Shi'i was a Muslim and possessed an Islamic world view. In his view, the essential was a shared religion and not a shared nationality, which he considered a disruptive force in religion. We see in the *Kitâb al-Naqz* [Book of Controvertion] that from one vantage point Shi'is were accused of being Zoroastrians:

> "Just as the Zoroastrians consider themselves the clients of the Sasanian dynasty, the Râfezite heretics [Twelver Shi'a] consider themselves the masters of the 'Alids. And just as the Zoroastrians consider the kingdom in terms of the *farr* [divine favor] of God, so too the Râfezite heretics consider the caliphate, employing the term *nass* [the "appointment" of Ali as leader of the Muslims] in place of *farr*. Likewise just as the Zoroastrians say that Kaykhosrow did not die and was taken to heaven and is alive and will descend again to earth to renew the Zoroastrian faith, the Râfezite heretic says that the hidden imam is alive and will come and strengthen the Shi'i faith and take over the world, and will have ('Ali's sword) Zulfeqâr with him so that he might kill all Muslims with it."[22]

In short, the indictment is that Shi'i beliefs derive from the Zoroastrian faith, the Sasanians, and from before that and that the Râfezites are Zoroastrians who follow the beliefs of their forefathers. The Shiite would not only reject this insult, but would argue: "Praising Zoroastrians is heresy and deviant behavior; and although the baseless tales honoring Rostam, Sorkhâb [Sohrâb], Esfandiyâr, Kâvus, Zâl, and the rest are a blasphemous rejection of the bravery and excellence of 'Ali, the Prince of the Faithful, such heresy persists."[23]

Here the nature of the Shi'i's ambiguous situation clearly shows itself. He is accused by opponents of having persisted in the beliefs of his own ancestors and community, of being "nationalistic" in religion; while, for his part, the Shi'i not only does not accept the charge, but considers the stories of ancient Iran blasphemous and a rejection of the bravery and superiority of 'Ali, i.e., in blatant contradiction of the Imam who is the manifestation of his belief and religion.

---

22. 'Abd al-Jalil Râzi, *Kitâb al-naqz, ma'ruf be ba'zi masâleb al-navâseb min naqz ba'zi fazâyeb al-Ravâfez* [Book of Controvertion], compiled by Mir Jalâloddin Armavi Mohaddes (1954), p. 444.

23. Ibid., p. 35

The Safavid religious scholar Majlesi (1628–1699, of whom more anon) says in his already cited *Wellspring of Life*: "The worst stories are stories based on lies, and true stories which involve idle talk and senseless things like the *Shâhnâmeh* and other stories of Magians and infidels. Some religious scholars have forbidden the reading of them."[24] Then Majlesi quotes Imam Mohammad Naqi and the Prophet to the effect that remembering 'Ali b. Abi Taleb is a form of worship, while listening to stories of lies and Magian tales is a sign of insincerity.

So, if the Shi'i was situated in a "national" position in political terms, his situation was otherwise in the matter of culture (which is primarily in the realm of self-awareness). Religion constituted his total cultural value system. In the matter of language and history, the language and history of religion alone had value. Any phenomenon beyond the pale of the cultural order of religion was beyond the circle of spiritual values. The same held for the history of Iran and the Persian language. Language might have a practical and mundane value in establishing relations and communication, and history for moral edification or the like. But they do not possess divine and religious validity (which is essential and holy). And we see that Shi'i religious scholars did not have anything to do with the Persian language until much later. Furthermore, Shi'i jurisprudence was compiled in the ninth and tenth centuries by the "Three Mohammads": Kulayni (d. 939), the author of *Kitâb al-kâfi* [Book of Sufficiency]; Abu Ja'far Mohammad b. Hasan b. Ali called Sheikh Saduq and famous as Ibn Babuyeh (d. 991), the author of *Man lâ yahzuruhu al-faqih* [Every Man His Own Jurisprudent]; and Abu Ja'far Mohammad b. Hasan b. Ali Tusi known as Shaykh al-Tâyifa (d. 1067), the author of *Tahzib al-ahkâm* [Refining of Rules] and *Istibsâr* [Search for Sight].[25] These four books are the four pillars of Shi'i jurisprudence. Their authors, leading religious scholars, were Iranian, one from Rayy, the second from Qom, and the third from Tus; they lived right in the period of the flowering of the Persian language and Iranian culture, and each authored numerous writings. The author of the *Book of Controvertion* attributes three hundred valuable writings to Ibn Babuyeh and more

24. Quoted in *Book of Controvertion*, p. 35, footnote.

25. [MH] Mohammad b. Ya'qub Kulayni, *Kitâb al-kâfi* [Book of Sufficiency] (Tehran, 1978-), translated by Mohammad Hasan Rizvi and edited by Mohammad Reza al-Ja'fari as al-Kâfi, Vol. 1, Part 1) *The Book of Excellence of Knowledge* (Karachi: Khorâsân Islamic Research Centre, 1978). On Kulayni, see Wilfred Madelung, "Abu Ja'far Muhammad al-Kulayni," *Encyclopaedia of Islam (New Edition)* 5 (1986): 362–363.

than two hundred volumes to Shaykh Tusi. But all of their writings are in Arabic, not in Persian. Elsewhere, *The Book of Controvertion* cites the names of Shi'i religious scholars from the cities of Qom, Nishâbur, Tus, Qazvin, Jorjân, Mashad, Kashan, Sâri, Zanjan, Mâmatir, Sabzevâr, Âstârâbâd, and smaller places such as Durvist of Nishâbur, Kisak of Rayy, Jâsp of Qom, Âbeh, Bekrâbâd, Dinâbâd, and Râvand,[26] all of whose works are in Arabic even though the authors lived in Persian-speaking environments.

In Safâ's words, "Twelver Shi'i authorship of books in Persian dated from the middle of the twelfth century, and the first valuable work of this sort in Persian is a book called *The Book of Controvertion* by Nasiroddin Abu al-Rashid 'Abd al-Jalil Râzi."[27] As far as we know, the first Shi'i commentary of the Koran in Persian is by Abolfotuh Râzi and dates from the twelfth century, two centuries after the appearance of Persian prose. After that, until the end of this period, books in Persian by Shi'i religious scholars are limited in number in comparison with other sorts of Persian books. Rare are works such as *Tabsirat al-'Awâmm fi Ma'rifat Maqâmât al-Anâm* [Advice to the People on the Knowledge of the Lofty Stages of Human Beings], on Twelver Shi'i beliefs, which was written in the thirteenth century in a simple, smooth prose.

Be that as it may, in this period Twelver Shiism was in a politically ambiguous situation with respect to nationality. But in cultural terms, Shi'i religious scholars had nothing to do with the Persian language, and not just Shi'i scholars, but religious scholars in general. In *Islam in Iran*, Petrushevskii cites the names of the authors of six major Sunni works of scholarship on Prophetic Traditions and six major Sunni commentaries on the Koran. All of the works are in Arabic, though the authors (except for two persons who are the author of one book) are all Iranians.

The Collapse of the Caliphal Center

In 1258 the Baghdad caliphate fell. For a period prior to this, that is, from the reign of Sultan Mohammad Khârazmshâh in the early years of the century, the relations of Iran with the caliphal court had deteriorated in all areas because of political differences. The occu-

---

26. 'Abd al-Jalil Râzi, *Book of Controvertion*.
27. Safa, *History of Literature in Iran*, vol. 2, p. 1033.

pation of Iran by the Mongols severed relations, and the fall of Baghdad into the hands of Hulagu, aided and abetted by Nasiroddin Tusi (1200–1274), brought the life of the caliphate to an end. The story of the Buyid conquest of Baghdad was this time repeated with the guidance of a Shiite and Iranian vizier, but with different events and consequences. Two famous Iranians, Nasiroddin Tusi and Sa'di, were on the scene. One had a hand in the demise of the caliphate, while Sa'di elegized it: "The sky has a right to weep tears of blood on the earth / At the downfall of the reign of Musta'sim, Prince of the Faithful." This itself seems a sign of the internal duality of our culture, which has manifested itself in the form of the confrontation of religious law and the Sufi way, Shiism and Sunnism, disciple and mentor, follower and religious source of emulation, and so on.

The Baghdad caliphate was the great base of Arab material and spiritual domination, of the domination of Arab government and culture. The destruction of this base reduced the power of Arabic and its capacity to spread, especially with the transfer of the political and administrative center to another place. In addition, because administrative affairs remained after the Mongol conquest in the hands of Iranians (but without the link with Arabic-speaking Baghdad), Persian became the single political and administrative language of Iran. The course of expansion of the Shi'i faith, which had commenced several centuries earlier, now proceeded at a faster pace. The tolerance and non-sectarianism of the Mongols and the wavering of the Il-Khans among the Buddhist, Christian, and Islamic faiths, and later the policy of the Timurids, as well as the elimination of the spiritual and material center of Sunnism in Baghdad, are further important factors in a complicated chain of various causes. On the subject of Shiism at the end of the Mongol age to before the advent of the Safavids, we would do well to refer to Ahmad Kasravi's scholarly essay, "Shaykh Safi and His Family." Kasravi writes:

> The seeds of Shiism had first been planted in Iran, and were it not for the victory of the Sunni Saljuqs, from those very first centuries Shiism would have proceeded to grow and would have achieved popularity throughout Iran. Thus it was that during the Mongol period, because there was freedom [of worship], Shiism automatically gained popularity in Iran. After the overthrow of the Mongols, Shi'i ruling dynasties appeared in this and that corner of Iran: the Sarbedârs in Khorâsân, the Mar'ashis in Mâzandarân, the

Keyânis in Gilan, the Mosha'sha' in Khuzistan and Lorestân, and the Qarra Qoyunlu in Azerbaijan, Iraq, and Fârs, each of whom in turn endeavored to promote Shiism. Tamerlane and his offspring also were closer to Shiism. It goes without saying that from the advent of these rulers, Shiism made great progress, especially since in those times the gap between Sunni and Shi'i was not as great as it is today.[28]

From the middle of the thirteenth century to the establishment of the Safavid state at the beginning of the sixteenth century, the Persian language of administration and the Twelver Shi'i faith both achieved greater currency and broader scope, while the nature of the relationship of the Shiites, as a religious minority, with the Sunni majority and both the local and central ruling government apparatus. But in this new social and religious situation, the "cultural" approach of Shi'i religious scholars remained generally unchanged, which is to say that Arabic remained the language of religion, with religious scholars continuing to write on the religious sciences in that language. In this context no significant change took place. Compared with the numerous writers of Persian prose on various subjects, the number of religious scholars writing in Persian was insignificant. In historiography, Sufism and social science or culture, this period featured such prominent figures as Rashidoddin Fazlollâh, Najmoddin Râzi, 'Aziz Nasafi, who wrote *Kitâb al-Insân al-Kâmil* [Book of the Perfect Man], Afzaloddin Kashani, Nasiroddin Tusi, Qotboddin Shirazi, 'Obayd Zakâni, and finally Sa'di. Opposite these masters, religious prose has, for example, the author of *Rowzat al-shohadâ* [Garden of Martyrs], Molla Hosayn Vâ'ez-e Kâshefi (d. 1504), who was not just a follower of the orthodox religious path, but also a Sufi. Scholars have expressed uncertainty about his religious affiliation: he is thought to be a Shi'i because of this book of his, and a Sunni because of his association with Mir 'Ali Shir Navâ'i and kinship with the poet Jâmi (1414–1492). In Dehkhoda's *Loghatnâmeh*, this entry appears after his name: "In Herat, where the people were Sunnis, he was accused of being a Shi'i; and in Sabzavâr, which was a center of Shiism, he was held in contempt and called a Sunni."[29] Moreover, the book is about the murders of martyrs and

28. Ahmad Kasravi, *Kârvand-e Kasravi* [Kasravi's Career], edited by Yahyâ Zokâ (Tehran, 1978), p. 85.

29. 'Ali Akbar Dehkhoda et al., "Vâ'ez Kâshefi," *Loghatnâmeh*, "Kâf" (Tehran: En-teshârât-e Majles-e Shurâ-ye Melli, 1957): 190–191.

imams, and not about religious sciences such as jurisprudence or theology. At any rate, if we come across the names of other religious scholars in this period who wrote in Persian on religious sciences and issues, their number is very small, and their works have no value as prose. One cannot compare them with the language of members of the court and Sufis of the same era, from Nasiroddin Tusi to Jâmi, much less with Nasafi and Sa'di. The "cultural politics" of the religious remained exactly as it had been.

Religious Prose in the Second Period (1501–1736)

Now we will consider religious prose in the second period of our chronology, that is, the period when Twelver Shiism is the majority faith and the official state religion. To be sure, in this period also for the reason already cited, so far as concerns Islam and its sects, the scholars of religion opposed the concept of nationality and rejected national thinking and culture. But political-social reality is another thing and, despite their beliefs, influenced their cultural development and altered their conduct in some areas.

The Safavid Shah Esma'il (ruled 1501–1524) became monarch of a country in which the majority of the people were Sunnis. He promulgated Shiism, which was the religion of the king and the Safavid government, through violence, fanaticism and the sword and made it the faith of the majority of the population. But from Safavid times onward, such tribal groups as the Kurds, Turkomans and Baluch have remained part of a significant Sunni population in Iran. Beyond its borders, Iran also faced two powerful Sunni enemies and engaged in lengthy wars with them: the Uzbeks in Transoxiana and the Ottomans in Turkey and Iraq. The wars with these two enemies did not have religious or sectarian causes. Conflict with the Uzbeks had begun before the Safavids, in the time of the Sunni Timurids. Whether Sunni or Shi'i, they wanted Khorâsân. The Ottoman Empire also was in a state of growth and expansion and did not recognize any limits for itself in any direction, not in Europe and not in Africa, except where it confronted an impenetrable barrier. To the east of the empire, in its confrontation with Iran, the situation was the same. The government of Iran, whatever it might be, had either to surrender or to fight, and the Safavids chose the second course.

Shiism and War with Iran's Neighbors

But the wars of the Safavids with the Uzbeks and the Ottomans assumed a religious coloring from the very start, not only because the "Sunni-slaying" Shah Esma'il was a harsh and merciless Shi'i, but also because his contemporaries, the Uzbek Shaybâni Khan and the Ottoman Sultan Selim were no less energetic and cruel in Shi'i-slaying, especially since the Ottoman sultans also claimed to be successors of the Prophet and the Muslim caliphate. On both sides, then, the war acquired a sectarian character. What is relevant to us is that the Safavids established a nationwide, monolithic state based on Twelver Shiism. And in their lengthy struggles both at home and abroad (to use today's terms) they needed an "ideology." Shiism came to serve as this ideology and became a "national" issue. Neither the Turkish-speaking Qizilbâsh tribes of Azerbaijan, northwest Iran and eastern Anatolia (which were the birthplace and, especially at first, the refuge of the Safavid government), nor the Safavid clan perceived themselves as of Iranian nationality. They had become intertwined with the history and culture peculiar to Iran by means of a form of popular Shiism and Sufism, but they did not even speak Persian. Nevertheless, official Safavid religious policy rendered a geographical region—Iran—not only distinctive from neighboring regions, but even identifiable as an entity in contrast with those other regions. This distinctiveness subconsciously served a sort of national feeling. This is one of those instances where, in Marx's words, men want to produce one thing, but in practice another history is constructed. In this case perhaps the course of events and happenstances was stronger than the architects of history and these subconscious forces played a more extensive role than conscious will, with the result that the Safavid state became possessed of a national coloring in religious and social terms.

Naturally the Shi'i jurisprudent or religious scholar did not believe in or accept a national role for Shiism. One could not devolve and delimit religion, which was a divine matter and a universal and eternal truth, to a national and exclusively mundane matter. As the deputy for the Twelfth Imam and the propagator of the true Twelver Shi'i faith, the Shi'i theologian was opposed to the government of Sunnis and consequently to Uzbek princes and Ottoman caliphs. His social role was revealed in religious form and was expressed in action. His conviction and action here coincided with the policy of the Safavid state; and, like it or not, the scholar of religion assumed a social and national role.

In fighting against the Uzbek khan and the Ottoman sultan and caliph, both the religious system and the governmental system became united as partners in a "religio-national" issue. This is a major difference in the social role of religious scholars of this period from that of earlier periods.

The Linking of Religious Institutions and the State

The legitimacy of the Safavids (1501–1736) became a matter of dispute from the middle years of the rule of this dynasty. According to John Chardin's report, in the years from 1660 to 1670 discussion and dispute arose over the issue of whether *mojtaheds* or descendents of the Prophet were the rightful successors to the Hidden Imam.[30] Nevertheless, in general, no division existed in this period between religion and government. The Safavid monarchs were at once sayyids, from the family of the Prophet, and Sufi mentors; both deputies of the Hidden Imam and the greatest of Sufis. In short, they had religious and worldly authority together. During the Battle of Chaldiran in 1614, Iranian soldiers attacked their Ottoman adversaries with the cry: "I testify that Esma'il is the legatee of God!"[31] Basically the popular Shiism of the mass of followers of the early Safavids provided scope for the appearance of hyperbolic images and even for fantasies of miracles and sainthood in the great Sufi.

In the extensive civil-religious Safavid system of government, scholars and other men of religion had official duties under various titles and different ranks and took part in the administration of the country, as a few examples of such offices indicate: *mollâbâshi* [chief mullah], *sadr-e khâsseh, sadr-e mamâlek, sadr-e 'âmmeh*, [religious magistrates], *mobâsherân-e owaâf* [superintendents of endowment foundations], *modarresân* [madraseh teachers], *shaykh ol-eslâm*, etc. In his Travel Diary, Engelbert Kaempfer, a very observant traveler to Safavid Iran, writes: "The State High Priest [= *sadr*], who is the most important source of interpretation and emulation for commentaries on Shi'i jurisprudence, is the leader of the clerics of Iran. He has the

---

30. Refer to J. Aubin, "La politique religieuse des Safavides," *Le Shi'isme imamite* (Paris: Presses Universitaires de France), p. 240. [MH] Sir John Chardin (1643–1713), *Travels in Persia* (1972, first printed in 1927).

31. Fereydun Garayeli, *Nishâpur, Shahr-e firuzeh* [Nishâpur, City of Turquoise] (Mashhad: Enteshârât-e Daneshgah-e Ferdowsi, 1978), p. 164.

same rank for Iranians that the Grand Mufti has for the Turks. But in addition he also has a high governmental position such that he has combined within his person religious and secular prerogatives. People in the street call him *navâb*, which has the approximate meaning of 'deputy of the shah.' The actual royal deputy, that is to say, the grand vizier, does not object to this title . . . The holder of this most lofty position arbitrates all of the legal claims presented in his presence free of any error in accordance with justice, in the popular view. Complaints to another court and requests for review with respect to his judgments is impossible . . . He who holds ultimate authority over all mosques, endowment foundations and holy places has the right to determine stipends and salaries for foundation custodians, employees and servants, teachers, theological students, preachers and clerics of all ranks at his own discretion in accordance with their efficiency. The king entrusts this highly paid position of the *sadr*, whom all clerics hold in respect, only to someone who has family ties of blood or marriage to him."[32]

The *sadr* and other positions cited were all in one way or another functionaries and stipend-holders of the state system. In these circumstances the Twelver Shi'i sect had, in addition to its "national" role, a broad governmental and administrative role which religious scholars and representatives of the religion had perforce to execute. And just as religious scholars came to have a national, governmental, and administrative role, they likewise became masters of the national, governmental, and administrative language, which was Persian. No longer was communication with followers solely religious and limited to matters of religious law that were all oral and could be carried out from the pulpit, mosque or cloister through sermons and addresses and responses. Nor was it restricted to "scientific" communication concerning religious science among religious scholars such as could be carried out in Arabic.

Persian Writings of Religious Scholars

For all of these reasons, religious scholars turned to the Persian language, but primarily, as might be expected, in order to propagate the faith, with all that it entails, from law, ethics, manners,

---

32. *Am Hofe des persisenen Grosskönigs*, p. 97; *Jahândâri, Safarnâmeh-ye Kempfer*, Jahândâri, pp. 121–2. For more information, see Nasrollâh Falsafi, *Zendegi-ye Shâh 'Abbâs* [The Life of Shah 'Abbâs].

trade, and earning a livelihood to politics, religious law, and superstitions. It is correct that they had in practice a national function by
virtue of their collaboration with the state. Yet their national function was primarily the preservation and promotion of a religion
which had become, through historical circumstances, a national
religion. They proceeded to write about religious problems in a
simple language "so that all people in all classes might profit and
benefit from reading."

The *Majâles al-mo'menin* [Gatherings of the Faithful] by Qâzi
Nurollâh Shushtari (though composed in India) and *Tafsir al-Zavâri*,
also called *Tarjomat al-Khavâs* (1539–40), a Koranic commentary in
simple language by 'Ali Hosayn Zawârehî, are among these works, as
is the sixteenth-century commentary called *Manhaj al-Sâdeqin* [Way
of the Truthful] by Mollâ Fathollâh b. Shokrollâh Kâshâni, which,
according to Motahhari, "was until thirty or forty years ago the only
commonly used Persian commentary."[33]

In addition to what has been said, Shiism in this period was the
domestic and foreign basis of the policies of Safavid monarchs. They
promoted the faith for political reasons. For such purposes the
language of the audience, which was Persian, had to be used. And
religious scholars did this for reasons already cited. The preface to the
Jâme'-e 'Abbâsi [Compendium of the Era of Shâh 'Abbâs] by Shaykh
Bahâ'oddin 'Âmeli (1547–1621), a prominent and influential religious
scholar of Shâh 'Abbâs's day and the Shaykh ol-Eslâm of Isfahan,
clearly shows one motive for writing Persian on the part of religious
scholars:

> Because the attention of the heavenward-gazing, the most noble and
> holy, the dog at the threshold of Imam 'Ali, Shâh 'Abbâs al-Hosayni
> al-Musavi al-Safavi Bahâdor Khan (whose noble name, may God
> perpetuate it, is manifest and obvious), is inclined to the
> dissemination of religious information and the promotion of spiritual
> knowledge, and the will of his holy Excellency is that all people and
> Shiites and servants of 'Ali, the Prince of the Faithful, be
> knowledgeable concerning the issues of the true religion and
> apprised of the rules and commands of the Holy Imams, God's
> prayers upon all of them; therefore, the blessed command has been
> issued that your servant, the suppliant Bahâ'oddin Mohammad
> 'Âmeli, prepare a book which would contain such necessary matters

33. 'Ali Hosayn Zavâreh, *Khadamât-e motaqâbel-e Eslâm va Irân* [Reciprocal Contributions of Islam and Irân] (Tehran: Enteshârât-e Sadrâ, 1980), p. 61.

of religion as ablutions before prayer, ceremonial washing, ablution with sand or dust, ritual prayer, almsgiving, *hajj*, *jihâd*, pilgrimages to the tombs of the Prophet, 'Ali and the other Imams, their birthdays and anniversaries of death, and other matters with respect to which needs routinely arise, for example, endowments, almsgiving, financial transactions, marriage, divorce, oaths, breaking oaths and vows, freeing slaves, determining blood money for the murder of a person, determining blood money for the loss of a limb and wounds which one person inflicts upon another, and the rules and ways reported of the Holy Imams with respect to eating food, drinking liquids, wearing clothes, hunting, and the like. In conformance with the most noble and lofty command, this book was written and its contents presented in idioms clear and near to the understanding so that everyone from upper to lower classes might find and derive benefit from reading it.[34]

As far as we know, Shaykh Bahâ'i's *Compendium of the Era of Shâh 'Abbâs* is the first comprehensive work of jurisprudence in Persian. Prior to it, treatises had been composed in Persian on various theological subjects, but not a book which presented all jurisprudential issues. This activity commences from an age when it is an extremely important event in terms of culture (in the broad sense of the word). It is a turning point.

Islamic jurisprudence is not law in the modern sense of the term. The philosophy of law, conception of the law, its appearance and implementation, the relevant social, historical and cultural conditions, debate and reasoning of their hows and whys . . . Islamic jurisprudence is all of these. But beside that, in jurisprudence the meaning of truth is not separate from religion and the spiritual world, from religious law, customs, traditions, and even other kinds of knowledge, such as medicine. This holds for the contents of the *Jâme'-e 'Abbâsi* as well. The book expounds transactions and contracts, buying and selling, manumission of slaves, ritual impurities and purities, retribution for wrongdoing, debts, punishments, rules of inheritance, marriage and divorce. Along with these appear rules for prayer, fasting, the *hajj* pilgrimage, alms, tithes, pilgrimages to the tombs of Imams and texts for pilgrimage prayers. Alongside such strictly legal matters appear issues of conduct and behavior, such as the rules for eating, sitting at meal times, washing hands and, in short, being a guest and being a

---

34. Bahâ'oddin 'Âmeli [Shaykh Bahâ'i], *Jâme'-e 'Abbâsi* [Compendium of the Era of Shâh 'Abbâs] (Tehran: Enteshârât-e Farâhâni), pp. 2–3.

host. The book's fifteenth chapter is "on the benefits of foods and the properties of fruits." By eating different kinds of meat, leaves of beets, *hariseh* [a meat and wheat dish], and grilled lentils . . . one can achieve, among other things, the following results: a cure for jaundice or hemorrhoids, control of vitiligo, increase in potency, sight, and hearing, increasing the number of one's children, quenching thirst, strengthening the gastric system, sensitizing the stomach, and increasing tears in the eyes.

Few things concerning this world and the next remained beyond the purview of the theologian's *ejtehâd* [exercise of judgment] and *fatwa* [edict]. What is particularly significant is that this manner of writing a book later became the model for Shi'i theologians. The tradition of scholarly treatises of this sort written today by leading clerics on theological matters as resources for emulation by the faithful reaches back to the Safavid period and follows this model or other examples, such as the works of Majlesi.

Mollâ Mohammad Bâqer Majlesi (1627–1698)

Persian writing by religious scholars reaches a culmination toward the end of the Safavid era, in particular with Mollâ Mohammad Bâqer Majlesi, the chief cleric in the royal court of Shah Soltân Hosayn (ruled 1694–1713). Majlesi authored some sixty works, all of which are in Persian except for a twenty-six-volume work in Arabic called *Bihâr al-Anwâr* [Seas of Lights] (c. 1694). Among his major works are: *Haqq al-Yaqin* [Truth of Certitude], on the principles of religion, *Hilyat al-muttaqîn* [Countenance of the Pure], on rules and customs, *Hayât al-qulûb* [Life of Hearts], on the history of the prophets, kings, and imams, *'Ayn al-hayât* [Wellspring of Life], on preaching, asceticism, and rejection of this world, *Zâd al-ma'âd* [Provisions for Resurrection] and *Jalâ al-'uyûn* [Luster of Eyes], on the history of the lives, vicissitudes, and miracles of the Shi'i Imams, *Tuhfat al-Zâ'er* [The Pilgrim's Souvenir], *Rabi' al-asâbî'* [Spring of the Weeks] and *Mishkât al-anwâr* [Lamp of Lights], on the perfection of the Koran, *Miqyâs al-masâbîh* [Standard of Lights] on performance of prayers, and numerous scattered treatises.[35] According to Bahâr's calculation, Majlesi composed

---

35. Dehkhoda et al., "Majlesi," *Loghatnâmeh*, "Mim" (Tehran: Tehran University Press, 1973): 466. [MH] For a sample of Majlesi's prose, see *Masâbîh* [Standard of Lights], translated by A.N. Matthews (Calcutta: Maulana Fazlul Karim, 1938–1939);

or commissioned approximately 1,202,700 couplets of verse on the Twelver Shi'i faith. In a lifetime of seventy-three years, this means the production of 19,210 couplets a year, each of which could contain ten words.[36]

The custom of writing about theological matters in simple language everyone could understand for use by the faithful began at the command of Shâh 'Abbâs I with Shaykh Bahâ'i (1547–1621). One can only guess the depth and breadth of the effects of this order on the spiritual and material lives, the cultural mentality and the day-to-day existence of the emulators, i.e., the majority of the people of Iran, who patterned their behavior in accordance with these treatises.

Because of this extraordinary influence of works by theologians on the faithful, I offer here a cursory look at one or two examples of the writings of Majlesi, who was the most important and prominent religious author of the Safavid period and, in all likelihood, the most prolific author in the history of Iran. My purpose here is to illustrate both the views of that influential and unique religious scholar of the later Safavid era on the subjects of law, religious law, religious rules and manners, science, Sufism and medicine, and also his easy-to-understand language and prose style.

In *Truth of Certitude*, Majlesi writes:

> Because the prophetic mission of Mohammad was not limited to his own age, but rather his is a prophetic mission for all of creation until Resurrection Day, for them he brought a book, and a body of religious law was laid down based on God's plan, rules and traditions on every matter, even on eating, drinking, sexual intercourse, and easing nature, and establishing religious precepts for ritual, inheritance, litigation, transactions, and decisions in accordance with divine truth.[37]

Majlesi has this to say about science:

> It is reported of Imam Musâ Kâzem that the Prophet of God declared that science consists of three sciences only, others being superfluous and of no use. The three are: knowledge of the clear, secure *âyeh*s [divine signs, verses in the Koran]; of the religious duties and

and *The Life and Religion of Mohammed as Contained in the Shee'eh Tradition of the Hyât-ul-Kuloob*, translated by J.L. Merrick (Boston, 1850).

36. Bahâr, *Study of Style*, vol. 3, p. 304.

37. Majlesi, *Haqq al-yaqîn* [Truth of Certitude] (Tehran: 'Elmi, 1956), p. 35.

obligations, which God has fixed in his justice; and of the Prophetic
Traditions, which are valid until the Day of Resurrection . . .
'It is necessary to study a science such that studying of it merits
divine approval and that it leads to eternal happiness, although it is
apparent that not every science leads to salvation . . . Beneficial
science which leads to salvation consists of those sciences that have
reached us from the members of the Prophet's family, because all
Koranic laws have been explained in Prophetic Traditions, and
commentaries on the bulk of analogous situations have reached us as
well. Reflection on some of those that have not thus reached us is not
good. And of other sciences, only that much is necessary which is
required for the understanding of their statements. Sciences beyond
that are useless and null and void, and a waste of one's life, or cause
the creation of likenesses or analogies in the soul which generally
lead to apostasy and heresy, in which case the likelihood of salvation
is remote.[38]

Majlesi's views on Sufis, love poetry, music and musical recitation
are likewise telling. After a lengthy exposition in *Wellspring of Life* of
ritual invocations of God by the Sufis, he says emphatically:

From these Koranic verses and Prophetic Traditions, it is clear that
this sort of yelling and repeated mentioning of God's name is
unacceptable according to religious law. Moreover, their writings,
songs, and invocations put to music, and their impious love poems
recited and set to music, all of this is forbidden in the view of our
religious scholars, as you learned in the section on music and song. . .
And dancing is forbidden by religious law, and reason leads every
person to the judgment that it is an abomination. Moreover, to do
these things in mosques and recite poetry there is forbidden.
According to a reliable report, the Prophet declared that if you hear
a person reciting a poem in a mosque, say to him: 'May God break
your mouth.' Mosques have been built for recitation of the Koran.
Furthermore, loud singing in mosques has been forbidden. The
majority of these people carry out these activities on Thursday
evening and Friday, whereas singing and poetry recitation are
absolutely disapproved on Thursday evening and disapproved for
Friday as well. When you tell them that these activities are
innovations challenging religious law, they answer that they achieve a
nearness to God through the activity, and they scream and foam at
the mouth like animals. As for achieving proximity to God, it has

38.   Majlesi, *'Ayn al-hayât* [Wellspring of Life] (Tehran: Sherkat-e sahâmi-ye Tab'-e
Ketâb, 1954), pp. 174–5.

been earlier made clear that these are things we imagine, whereas the path to God is limited to observance of religious law. O dear reader, there is no better testimony to the deviant innovation of these activities than the fact that not one Shi'i or Sunni or Sufi has produced a report to the effect that the Prophet of Islam or the Holy Imams or their close companions or the religious scholars of their people ever made use of a minstrel or that he hummed for them or that they formed a circle to recite litanies or that their companions followed that course. By the blessing of the family of the Prophet, you will abandon the reported one hundred thousand couplets of invocations, prayers, litanies, repetitions, and incantations, and the shameless incantations which some Sunnis have compiled, you will not recite, for they are lacking in significant sense, and in terms of Arabic grammar most of them are full of errors.'[39]

A consideration of Majlesi's prose appears at the end of this discussion. Before that, it is appropriate to consider these works in terms of the decisive and profound effects they have had on our social life and history. From the broad scope of the science of jurisprudence one can appreciate how it circumscribes the various contexts of human life. Naturally, the expert who disposes of the right to command and to reject in these contexts is a person who has attained *ejtehâd* [exercise of judgment] in this science, i.e., a jurisprudent. Just as the despotic Safavid monarch disposes of the lives and property of his subjects, religious scholars own the souls and faith of the faithful. The sultan and the jurisprudent are compeers and complement one another in rule over humanity in this world and in the next. From this age onward, jurisprudents and religious scholars considered themselves the sole possessors of the right to guide and intervene in the various matters of the life of the people, especially since they are the successors to the Hidden Imam and the religious leaders of the faithful. Because of this also, Majlesi, the renowned jurisprudent and religious scholar, the chief cleric in the royal court and undisputed possessor of prerogatives in the realm, later became the model for other jurisprudents and religious scholars.

Now let us look at his influence and guidance in other contexts. The book called *Countenance of the Pure* states as its subject "the exposition of virtues of proper behavior," from wearing clothes to sexual intercourse and association with females, clipping fingernails, sleeping, waking, urination and defecation, enemas, sneezing, entering and

---

39. Ibid., pp. 240–4.

leaving a domicile, and treatments and cures for many illnesses and diseases. The seventh chapter of the fifth section is "on plucking nasal hairs and playing with one's beard." The sixth chapter of the eleventh section treats "proper ways of sneezing, belching, and spitting." The headings alone of the ninth section are illustrative.

The Ninth Section: On bloodletting, enemas, and some herbs and spices and the remedies for some diseases and citation of some incantations and charms.

Chapter 1: On the spiritual rewards of illness and patience while ill, and an account of the intensity of the affliction of the faithful.

Chapter 2: On the virtues of bloodletting.

Chapter 3: On the types of medical treatment which the imams introduced and an explanation of the permissibility of recourse to physicians.

Chapter 4: On the types of cures and remedies.

Chapter 5: On universal prayers and incantations and compound mediations.

Chapter 6: On curing headaches, aches in the temples, head colds, epilepsy, disorders of the brain, and possession by jinn.

Chapter 7: On the curing of other illnesses and pains of the head and throat.

Chapter 8: On the cure of scrofulous conditions, sores, wounds, boils, cankers, vitiligo, leprous conditions, freckles and moles, and the like.

Chapter 9: On curing internal ailments, colic, gas, stomach pains, and coughing.

Chapter 10: On remedies for arthritis of the joints, paralysis, hemorrhoids, diseases of the bladder, and other illnesses.

Chapter 11: A description of a few amulets against sorcery, poisons, bites, and other misfortunes.

Chapter 12: On the curative properties of the holy dust from Imam Hosayn's shrine, and the special properties of some herbs and spices.

The special importance of the book lies in the fact that all of these discussions have a religious aspect. Majlesi wrote the book on the strength of Prophetic Traditions and reports (*hadith*). The openings of the twelve chapters of this section are as follows:

–It is reported in a reliable tradition from Imam Ja'far Sâdeq that . . .

–On the basis of a reliable report from Imam Ja'far Sâdeq it is reported that . . .

–It is reported of the Prophet that . . .

–It has been recorded in many Traditions that . . .

–In a reliable Tradition from Imam Sâdeq it is reported that . . .

–It is reported of Imam Mohammad Bâqer that . . .

–In a reliable Tradition from 'Ali, Prince of the Faithful, it is reported that . . .

–It is reported from 'Ali b. No'mân that he petitioned Imam Rezâ that . . .

–A reliable Tradition reports that . . .

–A reliable Tradition reports that 'Ali, Prince of the Faithful . . .

–In many reliable Traditions it is reported that a cure for every pain is to be had in the dirt from the grave of Imam Hosayn . . .[40]

All of the discussions, instructions and rules in the book are based on the words and deeds of the Holy Ones, the Prophet and the Imams. Thus *Countenance of the Pure* is not just a book on the virtues of rules and manners, but rather it treats Islamic behavior in general and for many Shi'is it possessed, and possesses, the character of religious obligation.[41] What a great difference there is between the Islam of Majlesi and that of Rumi, who says: "We took the kernel of the Koran / And threw the husk to the donkeys." Not for nothing would divinity students in the Safavid era pick up Rumi's *Masnavi* with tongs so that their hands might not get contaminated, while the unfortunate Mollâ Sadrâ took refuge in a cave.

Medicine and the treatment of the sick by recourse to Prophetic Traditions and reports has a long history with us and is based on Shi'i jurisprudential sources, among them Kulayni's *Book of Sufficiency*, whose

---

40. Majlesi, *Hilyat al-muttaqîn* [Countenance of the Pure].

41. Safavid Shiism was initially an admixture of religious beliefs, superstitions, and Sufi ideas of popular origin among the people in the north and northwest of today's Iran. Their belief in the divinity of Shah Esma'il as a perfect guide is an example. The superstitious element of this religion reaches its apogee in this period with Majlesi. [MH] For a Shi'i clerical introduction to Twelver Shiism, see Sayyid Muhammad Husayn Tabâtabâ'i, *Shiite Islam*, translated from the Persian and edited and introduced by Sayyid Hossein Nasr (Albany, NY: SUNY Press, 1978). On Shi'i folk beliefs, there is Bess Donaldson, *The Wild Rue* (Mashhad, 1938).

chain of documentation reaches back to Imam Ja'far Sâdeq. From the
time of Majlesi, the jurisprudent's influence in affairs is such that not
only does he deal with medicine in the treatment of every ailment, but
also (as appears in the title of the third chapter of *Countenance of the
Pure*) the patient's recourse to a physician is, by religious law, dependent upon his permission. A study of Majlesi's works shows that, with
great effort and diligence, he introduced into Shiism, amongst other
things, a mass of superstitions.

The Style of Religious Treatises

Although the language of religion and government during the Safavid
Era was Persian, the language of the military and the court was Turkish,
this being the language of both the royal family and the Qizilbâsh
tribes which constituted the army.[42] Only from the time of Shâh 'Abbâs
I (1587–1629) were Persian speakers added to the army. Literature,
and especially Persian poetry, were not well regarded by Safavid
monarchs, both because the court language was Turkish, and because
they encouraged elegies of the Shi'i Imams as evidence of royal piety.
They did not support panegyrics for a king who represented himself
as "the dog at 'Ali's threshold." In fact, panegyric verse in the manner
of earlier court poets no longer existed. And the classics of the Persian
language, if not forgotten, no longer received attention and passed less
from mouth to mouth and hand to hand.

In addition, because of the influence of the court and the dispersal
of the Qizilbâsh leaders and their government throughout the land,
among other factors, the official Persian prose of this period was ugly,
full of Turkish words, inexpressive in terms of meaning, and confused
and in a sense vulgar in terms of structure. It was also impoverished in
terms of content and mostly restricted to history, official correspondence and government documents. It was a vulgar prose because it did
not have behind it a study of, and acquaintance with, the works of the
masters. At the same time, because it sought to mirror the splendor
and grandeur of the monarchy and the government, it became artificial,
exaggerated and pretentious.

In contrast, religious prose, especially that of Majlesi, was simple
and unadorned in terms of language. All the efforts of this prose

---

42. E. Kaempfer, *Am Hofe des persisenen Grosskönigs*, p. 134; Jahândâri, *Safarnâmeh-ye
Kempfer*, p. 168.

became devoted to the explanation of its aim, nothing more and nothing less. It did not stray from its practical and straightforward purpose. Consequently, it was not unlike much journalistic prose, which seeks to communicate the writer's view to the reader as simply and directly as possible. Majlesi's prose, moreover, with its great volume, was hurried, again like journalistic prose today. In contrast, *The Book of Government* shows that Nezâmolmolk (d. 1092), despite his many duties and responsibilities at court, had command of a wonderful Persian. But Majlesi's writings illustrate how religious and governmental duties kept the writer from knowledge of language. His language was untidy and not free of grammatical and other errors. Majlesi lived in an age of evanescence of Persian. His market-place language furthered this decline. His prose, of course, has other features as well, which are both characteristic of the language of religious scholars and observable in practically every period, an issue I shall return to at the end of this discussion. But let us now consider the language of science in the third period of our chronological classification, namely, from the end of the Safavid era to the rise of the Constitutional Movement.

A Look at the Development of Shiism

With the fall of Isfahan in 1722 to Sunni Afghân control, most of the religious scholars fled from that city to the shrine cities of Baghdad, Karbala, and Najaf. Nâder Shah Afshâr (ruled 1736–1747) not only had no affection for these Shi'i religious scholars, but was himself a Sunni and pursued a different religious policy. Discussion of this would sidetrack us from our own subject; here let me just mention that he eliminated the position of *sadr*, transformed the bulk of the endowments of mosques and religious schools into crown lands, and reduced the clerics and custodial authorities of such pious foundations to hard times. Nâder Shah "one day in Isfahan, summoning the Sadr al-Sodur, who supervised the stipends and pensions connected with pious foundations, asked him: 'What is the explanation for this limitless wealth you scholars and clerics have received and by what right do you dispose of it?' The sadr responded: 'Because we are supplicants of the king's government and because the permanence of religion and government depends upon our prayers.' To this Nâder Shah replied: 'How can you say that your prayers are accepted or granted? If your prayers were efficacious, you would not have fallen into the hands of the Afghâns.' "[43] Afterwards, Nâder added that conquering enemies depends upon the swords and hands of warriors, to whom this wealth properly belongs. He consequently ordered the confiscation of the wealth of the religious foundations.

At the Moghân conference in 1736, one of the conditions Nâder set for accepting the crown was that the Iranian people give up their Shiism and their animosity toward the [first three] caliphs. When the *mollâ-bâshi* [chief cleric] Mirzâ 'Abdolhosayn objected, Nâder ordered him suffocated to death.

The self-interested and despotic Nâder was never able to create a central government or a government structure. He himself constituted the government and the nation and managed government affairs like a headstrong tribal chief. The succeeding government of the Zands had a regional rather than national quality and lasted only a short time, not much more than the reign of Karim Khan Zand (from 1751 to 1779). Afterwards came widespread civil strife and war. The reign of Âghâ Mohammad Khan (ruled 1796–97), the founder of the Qajar dynasty, consisted of war, military expeditions and the establishment of a government over the whole country.

In this period Isfahan, earlier the political and religious center of Shiism, gradually relinquished its position to Karbala and Najaf. This movement of the center of Shiism out of the Iranian monarchical realm led to greater practical freedom in the relationship of religious scholars and teachers with the Iranian faithful and to open involvement on the part of clerics with national affairs.

In this relatively short period from the fall of Isfahan to the beginning of the reign of Fath 'Ali Shah (1797–1834), Shiite leaders had no role in political and governmental affairs. As for internal Shi'i politics, theoretical and practical control was in the hands of "Akhbâri," as opposed to "Osuli," teachers and scholars. "The *Akhbâri* scholar or relator of Prophetic Traditions is a person who believes that the documentation and premises of jurisprudential interpretation do not extend beyond the Koran and the Traditions. The *Osuli* scholar accepts two

---

43. Mohammad Mahdi b. Mohammad Rezâ al-Esfahâni, *Nesf-e jahân fi ta'rif-e Esfahân* [Half the World, a Description of Esfahân], edited by Manuchehr Sotudeh (Tehran: Ta'yid and Amir Kabir, 1961), p. 257.

additional principles as well: reason and consensus, which he invokes in supporting his arguments at the stage of interpreting a legal edict.'[44]

But in this very period of the supremacy of the Akhbâris were sown the seeds of their defeat, with the birth of Mohammad Bâqer b. Mohammad Akmal Behbahâni. He was born in Isfahan a few years before the invasion of the Afghans. Apparently at the age of eighteen he left that city for Najaf. After further theological training in Behbahân, he settled in Karbala and commenced a fierce opposition to the Akhbâris, dealt definitively with them and established the ideological and practical supremacy of the Osuli religious scholars. For this reason he is called the "rejuvenator of the Shi'i faith."[45]

The definitive defeat of Mohammad Amin Astarâbâdi and his followers, and the theoretical and practical victory of the Osuli leaders under the leadership of Mohammad Bâqer b. Mohammad Akmal Behbahâni is very important in the history of Shiism because, for the Akhbâris, the exercise of *ejtehâd* has no place. One can derive legal judgments only from the Koran and Prophetic Traditions; whereas Osuli scholars expand the *mojtahed*'s circle of legal interpretation, bringing reason and consensus to the fore. Consequently the theologian possesses freedom of action in broader contexts.

The question of spiritual authority, the relation between leader and follower, and the control of the qualified *mojtahed* over the material and spiritual affairs of believers achieves its final form in this period. Shaykh Mohammad Hasan, author of the famous theological work called *Javâher al-Kalâm* [Jewels of Speech, or Pearls of Theology], Shaykh Mortaza Ansâri and Mirzâ Shirâzi were among the first theologians to possess total authority in terms of imitation (by the faithful of their directives). Prior to them neither Shaykh Bahâ'i nor Majlesi nor Shaykh Saduq nor 'Allâmeh Helli held such authority over the faithful. Besides this separation of religious organizations from the government at a period in which Shiism was the official religion of the country, Shi'is also became independent in financial and administrative

---

44. Mahmud Shehâbi, "Dibâcheh" [Preface], *Taqrirât-e osul* [Declarations of Principles] (Tehran: Tehran University Press, 1956), p. "md." For information on the Akhbâri scholars in the seventeenth and eighteenth centuries and differences between them and Osuli scholars, refer to 'Ali Davâ'i, *Ostâd-e koll Vahid Behbahâni* [Master Vahid Behbahâni] (Qom: Châpkhâneh-ye Dâr al-'Elm, n.d.), pp. 75, 95.

45. Mohammad b. Solaymân al-Tonokâboni, *Qesas al-'olamâ* [Stories of Religious Scholars], second edition, 1925.

affairs, for example in the payment of the imam's share, the tithe and religious taxes to religious authorities, and the nonpayment of taxes to the government. Of course the way for this development was paved and solidified in earlier centuries. But in this period religious scholars and teachers were able to separate their own expenses and religious institutions from a government that was of the same religion. From this period the theoretical and practical context became further prepared for the rivalry and outright power struggle between the two forces of government and religion, between ruler and theologian. The later ups and downs of this rivalry depended upon the power and weakness of the two parties and other social conditions. At any rate, during the Qajar era, especially from the reign of Fath 'Ali Shah to the end of the Constitutional Movement (1911), the Shi'i clergy played a role in practically all of the major events of fundamental importance, such as the wars between Iran and Russia and in the tobacco boycott.

Examples of Writing by Religious Scholars

Active clerical participation in the country's political and social life should naturally have led to reflection or discussion of these issues in the works of religious scholars of the period. But titles of works by leading religious scholars of the age show that their preoccupations at the end of the eighteenth century were otherwise. My source listing Qajar era writings by religious scholars is the book called *Stories of Religious Scholars* (1925, second printing), whose author is Mohammad Ebn-e Solaymân al-Tonokâboni, himself an Usuli theologian, who wrote his book in 1911.

1–The Writings of Shaykh Mortazâ Shushtari Ansâri: The treatises *Asl-e barâ'at* [Principle of Innocence], *Resâleh-ye estes'hâb* [Treatise on Confirmation], *Resâleh-ye tarâjih* [Treatise on Preferences], *Resâleh-ye qor'eh* [Treatise on Lots], *Resâleh-ye taqiyeh* [Treatise on Dissimulation], *Resâleh-ye raf'-e zarar* [Treatise on Compensation of Loss] and *Sharh-e tahârat Ketâb-e ershad-e 'allâmeh va motâjer* [Ritual Purification: Book of Guidance for Scholar and Merchant] were composed independently as volumes. Miscellaneous notes in the book called *'Avâyed* [Profits] by Hâji Mollâ Ahmad Narâqi were actually about the principles of jurisprudence, i.e., were based on the proof of conjecture and the principles of exemption and confirmation.

2–The writings of Aqâ Sayyid Mohammad (who issued the edict of *jihâd* [holy struggle] against the Russians): *Jâme' ol-'abâyer* [Compendium of Maxims and Anecdotes] . . . "one volume of it, which is a discussion of ablutions in the case of sexual intercourse and ejaculation, is in my possession and the discussion of ablution exceeds seventy volumes. *Mafâtih al-osul* [Keys to Principles] on the elements of jurisprudence, consisting of 40,000 verse couplets or more. The book called *Manâhel* [Fountains] on jurisprudence . . . of nearly 20,000 couplets or more. The book *Masâbih* [Lantern Lights] on jurisprudence; the book *Eslâh ol-'amal* [Rectification of Action], all famous works on jurisprudence; *Aklil al-masâ'eb* [Bouquet of Hardships]. Aqâ Mohammad Shafi' Borujerdi has written that he heard Aqâ Sayyid Mohammad say that his writings perhaps exceeded 300,000 couplets." The author of *Reports of Religious Scholars* states that his own oeuvre exceeds that quantity and, indeed, is greater than one million couplets and Hâji Mohammad Sâleh Borghani, who was a student of Sayyid Mohammad, stated that among recent writers no one had written more than his master Sayyid Mohammad and that he produced six compilations in the course of twenty-four hours.[46]

3–The writings of Hojjat ol-Eslâm Hâji Sayyid Mohammad Bâqer Shafti: *Matâle' al-anvâr* [Rising Places of Lights], "which is an explanation of prayers based on religious laws consisting of seven volumes which do not exhaust the subject, each volume containing approximately 20,000 couplets"; the treatise called *Zahrat al-Bareqa* [Flower of Illumination], which treats several issues of vocabulary in the science of juridicial principles; the treatise *Tohfat al-abrâr dar salât* [Treatise on the Marvels of Prayer for the Pious]; the biographies *Resâleh dar bayân-e hâl-e Es'hâq b. 'Omar, Resâleh dar ahvâl-e Ebrâhim b. Hâshem Qomi, Resâleh dar tahqiq-e hâl-e Mohammad b. 'Isâ al-Yaqtini, Resâleh dar bayân-e hokm-e 'aqd bar okht-e motlaqah* [Exposition of Matrimonial Law for the Divorcee], *Resâleh dar qabul-e qowl-e nesvân be kholov az mavâne'-e nikâh* [Treatise on the Acceptance of Women's Testimony in Private without Compromising Them].

4–The writings of Mollâ Ahmad Narâqi are a final illustration: Three books on *osul* (juridicial principles); *Me'raj ol-sa'âda* (Ascension to Felicity, Persian translation); *Sayf ol-Omma* (The Sword of the [Muslim] Community in refutation of the doubts of a Christian friar); *'Avâ'ed ol'Ayyâm* (Accruals of the Days), on the general rules of juris-

---

46. al-Tonokâboni, *Stories of Religious Scholars*, pp. 91-92.

prudence; a book in closed couplets called *Tâqdis*, and *Mostamad ol-Shi'a* (The Documented Basis of Shiism.)

Besides their spiritual and religious standing, these religious scholars were among the most influential men in the society of their day. Examples are Mollâ Ahmad Narâqi and Aqâ Sayyid Mohammad, who had a leading role in the edict of *jihâd* and the declaration of war between Iran and Russia.

Mollâ Ahmad Narâqi's famous book called *Me'râj ol-sa'âda*, which is "on the science of ethics and Islamic customs and traditions," is a translation of "*Ham al-Sâdât*, [Forebear of Sayyids], the work of the noble, respected parent" of the translator. In his preface, after praising God, the prophet and the Imams, Mollâ Ahmad Narâqi describes Fath'ali Shah in these words:

> "His Majesty, the King, who sits on the throne of Jamshid, whose army comprises angels, whose court is celestial, the *khedive* of the age, the *qibla* of the world's sultans and the leader of khans of the ages, the founder of the basis of religion and the promoter of the religion of the Lord of the Prophets, the beautiful signature of caliphal firmans and the splendor of the beauty of the perfection of the kingdom, the shining sun of the firmament of monarchy, the glowing orb in the sphere of glory, the obliterator of the memorials to tyranny and enmity, the manifestation of God's injunction to justice and charity, a Chosroes the likes of whom the stars, though they have become all eyes, have never seen in centuries of conjunctions; a Tamerlane whose dangerous conquests the old firmament, though it has become all body and ears, has never heard . . . he has kept the heart and soul of the kingdom free from the contamination of wicked westerners, he has brought into his grasp the realm of the kingdom of ethics like the kingdoms of the four quarters of the world."[47]

This is a sample of the prose of the preface. Of course, the language of the text is simpler than this "royal" preface. As for its contents, the book treats a wide variety of subjects, even zoology and anatomy. For example, on the marvels of the creation of the mosquito "which, despite its small size, God made in the shape of the elephant, the largest of animals, and gave it a trunk like an elephant's trunk and created for it all the limbs elephants have, with the addition of two wings and two horns." Or on the marvels of the human skull, about

---

47. "Dibâcheh," *Me'râj ol-sa'âda* [Ascension to Bliss] (Tehran: Jâvidân), pp. 4, 5.

which Narâqi says that God "created it from six bones; two of them are in place of a roof, and the other four function as doors, and he linked all of them to each other, and the locus of their joining, which they call *sho'un* [dignity, rank] has numerous crevices so that the vapors which accumulate at the nose can escape outside . . ."[48] Likewise on the marvels of eye and ear, on the marvels of the human countenance or the stomach, heart, hands and fingers.

The writings of Mollâ Mahdi Narâqi, Mollâ Ahmad's father, also comprise various fields, for example, jurisprudence, the principles of jurisprudence, ethics, theology, cosmology, the sufferings of the Holy Family, rhetoric, the nature of existence, the rites of the Hajj pilgrimage, and the imamate.[49]

In Mortazâ Motahhari's words, this father and son "are leading figures among the religious scholars of Islam and both are famous for their catholicity of interest."[50]

Scholarly Style from the Safavid Period Onward

The Safavid tradition of religious scholarship, particularly that inspired by Majlesi, continued through the Qajar era (1796–1925) and remains alive and more active than ever today. Scholarly treatises by mojtaheds with followers and by celebrated scholars of our own age demonstrate that in almost all arenas of life, the Shi'i faithful obtain their orders and daily recipes for behavior from the leading religious scholars of the age. These are the rules pertaining to food and drink, and the rules for remedies and cures, enemas and vomiting, inheritance and hunting, cleansing after urination and defecation, ritual impurity, and every other thing.[51]

The Persian writing of religious scholars achieved general currency from the Safavid period onward. A number of treatises by religious scholars of this age, among them the treatises on practical matters by

48. *Ascension to Bliss*, pp. 94, 98.

49. 'Abdorrahim Kalântar Zarrâbi, *Târikh-e Kâshân* [History of Kâshân], edited by Iraj Afshâr (Tehran, 1977), p. 281.

50. Mortazâ Motahhari, as quoted in Kalântar Zarrâbi, *History of Kâshân*, p. 595.

51. [MH] A representative treatise in English is Ruhollah Khomeini's *Clarification of Questions: An Unabridged Translation of Resâleh Towzih al-Masael*, translated by J. Borujerdi, foreword by M.M.J. Fischer and Mehdi Abedi (Boulder, CO: Westview Press, 1984).

mojtaheds with followers, are in Persian. In this context there is change or development in the tradition of writing, from Arabic to Persian. But on the subject of the treatises, the traditional way of thinking, whether in Arabic or Persian, remains untouched. The spirit of discourse not only undergoes no evolution, it would appear to suffer retrogression. In terms of both content and form, this prose follows the language of Majlesi and Safavid religious scholars, as already discussed. *The Accounts of Religious Scholars* and the *Ascension to Felicity* illustrate the religious prose of this period, with their vulgar, ugly and sometimes flawed language, which is not even comparable with the court and administrative prose of the same period—though governmental prose is confused, undeveloped and imitative enough.

Especially from the Safavid era onward, in writing pertaining to jurisprudence or ethics and ceremonies, religious scholars entered into all private and public, individual and social arenas and contexts, explaining rules and clarifying the duties of the faithful. But in the political realm they infrequently engaged in theoretical and intellectual discussion. Or they avoided the subject altogether, and limited their involvement to daily political events, more often in the form of issuing necessary edicts, for example, in the war between Iran and Russia, the tobacco boycott, and the Constitutional Movement.

Political philosophy, the role of the state, its relation to individuals, their duties and obligations with respect to one another, social organizations and their roles, the system of government and political regimes, first come to the fore in the publications of religious scholars after the enactment of the Constitution and in the famous treatise by Shaykh Mohammad Hosayn Nâ'ini called *Tanbih al-umma wa tanzih al-milla* [Chastisement of the Community and Purification of the Nations]. This is one of those rare works about politics by a religious scholar.[52] The treatise was written shortly after the victory of the Constitution and in defense of it and its compatibility with religious law. In comparison with the works of intellectuals and liberals of the age on the subject of political rights and the law (for example, *General International Law* by Sâdeq Hazrat, *International Law* by Mirzâ

---

52. [MH] Shaykh Mohammad Hosayn Nâ'ini, *Tanbih al-umma wa tanzi al-milla*, introduced and annotated by Sayyid Mahmud Tâleqâni (Tehran). The most famous political essay by a Shi'i religious scholar is Ruhollâh Khomayni's *Hokumat-e Eslâmi* [Islamic Government] (Najaf, 1971?); translated into English by Joint Publications Research Service as *Islamic Government* (New York: Manor Books, 1979).

Mohammad 'Ali Khan Zokâ al-Molk), the useful and respectable treatise of this liberal religious scholar has little value, and on the subject of the philosophy of democratic government and constitutionalism does not match those other works.[53]

In fact, although the book is in Persian, it was conceptualized in Arabic. The structure of the language, the syntax of sentences, and the vast majority of the vocabulary and some of the rules of grammar are Arabic, as if Nâ'ini had written the book in Arabic and then translated it into bad Persian. It exhibits "Arabic-stricken" language. As an illustration, here is a passage from the book's preface:

> Know that this is accepted as certain by all nations and that all intelligent people in the world are in agreement, that if order in the world and mankind's search for livelihood are founded on monarchy and statecraft, whether it be by a single individual or a collective body, and whether its incumbent be lawfully established or despotically, whether by inheritance or by election, it is necessarily obvious that the preservation of the dignity and independence of every people, too, whether it concerns religious entitlements or national, is contingent upon the insurgence of their own sovereignty, of its own accord; otherwise considerations of entitlement and the mighty name of religion and confession and the honor and independence of their motherland and national identity will be totally annihilated. However high the degrees of wealth and power, and whatever prosperity and progress they might attain for the country, it is because in the holy religious law the preservation of the seed of Islam has been declared to be the most important of all duties, and the preservation of Islamic sovereignty to be among the duties and of the imamate.[54]

Here are several sentences from the first chapter which give a clearer impression of Nâ'ini's prose.

> Chapter One—On the exposition of the first matter, and discussion on it is in two stages: First on the exposition of the principal of limitation of arbitrary domination and monarchy in all religious legal systems and religions, with the adducing of those very necessary duties and preferred courses of action of the pertinent sort.

53. For more information, see Fereydun Adamiyat, sections 8 and 9, *Ideolozhi-ye nahzat-e mashrutiyat-e Irân* [Ideology of the Iranian Constitutional Movement], vol.1 (Tehran: Payâm, 1976).

54. Nâ'ini, *Chastisement of the Community*, p. 6.

Two—On the discovery of the degree of this limitation and its reality.

As for the first matter: From what transpired in the Preface, it is apparent and clear. That is to say that once you appreciate that the principle in establishing a kingdom and a strong order and the imposition of taxes *et alia* are all for the preservation and order of the country and for the shepherding of the flock and the education of the species and maintenance of the populace, and not for slaking of lusts and the realization of the aims of human-devouring wolves and the subjugation and enslavement of the people under self-willed desire, inevitably arbitrary government will be seen to consist, under every religious law and indeed in the view of every reasonable person, whether it was empowered by right or by force, in the safeguarding of persons and trusteeship of civil order and the preservation and the adducing of the other duties pertaining to custody, not a means for the use of force and proprietorship in accordance with the self-willed domination of territory and people, and that in truth it partakes of the nature of the custodianship of a pious foundation for them, for the management and preservation of a common endowment and the settlement among owners of rights and the remittance to each possessor of right of his own due.[55]

Such strange Persian, and yet contemporary with the prose of 'Ali Akbar Dehkhoda (1879–1956) and other writers of the Constitutional period! This problem, although not so pronounced, exists in the writing of religious scholars in all periods. In writing, they are more familiar with the Arabic language than with Persian. For this same reason their Persian frequently has the color and atmosphere of false Arabic. Especially for the Safavid period and for a time afterwards, when the study of classical Persian had been abandoned, this Arabicization of the Persian writing of religious scholars is more in evidence.

Also instructive in this regard is Hasan Taqizâdeh's view about the prose of Sayyid Jamâloddin Asadâbâdi [Afghâni] (1838–97), the leading statesman among religious scholars and the founder, according to some, of the Islamic movement. In Taqizâdeh's words: "In Persian, both in writing and in speaking, he had an Arabic and perhaps Afghan accent and style. His written Persian especially leads me almost to doubt that he was an Iranian."[56]

---

55. Ibid., pp. 42–43.
56. Hasan Taqizâdeh, *Kâveh* 2 (new series), no. 3.

At the same time Taqizâdeh's prose, and that of Mohammad Qazvini more so, because of their religious training, never freed itself of the tyranny of Arabic language and vocabulary. Outstanding scholars in their own realms, they both wrote atrocious Persian. When Ahmad Kasravi, another scholar who likewise was a theology student in his youth, sought to rid Persian of the influence of Arabic in line with his national and religious beliefs, he moved from one extreme to another and wrote *fârsi-ye sareh* [pure Persian]. One of the motives behind his "pure Persian" was a reaction to the *'arabi-ye sareh* [pure Arabic] of religious scholars from the later Safavid era onward.[57]

Another characteristic of the prose of the religious scholars in almost all periods is its pulpit style. The writers of these works are practitioners of sermons and addresses and speeches from the *menbar* [mosque rostrum]. They were the practitioners more of oral discourse than of written. We see this characteristic of prose from Abolfotuh's *Commentary* to *The Book of Controvertion* and *The Garden of Martyrs* and in the works of Majlesi and Mollâ Ahmad Narâqi, and in a pronounced manner in Jowhari's *Tufân al-bokâ* [Storm of Tears], a book of *rowzeh* sermons in a mixture of verse and prose. At its best, the prose of religious scholars exhibits the influence of religious sermons and the resonance of eloquence, and at its worst, the oversimplification and repetitious concatenations of *rowzeh* sermons.

In general our religious prose, except in Koranic commentaries, in which Persian discourse often reaches high points, does not achieve an exalted position. It remains a rudimentary vehicle of communication for meeting ordinary needs, perhaps for two reasons. One is that in jurisprudence, ethics, rules and rituals, religious legal experts dealt more with daily problems and issues, not with manifestations of the soul and soaring spiritual flights. The other is that, for them, language and literary culture in the full sense of the term was Arabic, while

---

57. [MH] The following essays offer critical assessments of this social and language reformer: M.A. Jazayery, "Kasravi's Analysis of Persian Poetry," *International Journal of Middle Eastern Studies* 4 (1973): 190–203; Asghar Fathi, "Kasravi's Views on Writers and Journalists: A Study in the Sociology of Modernism," *Iranian Studies* 19 (1986): 167–182; Amin Banani, "Ahmad Kasravi and the 'Purification' of Persian: A Study in Nationalist Motivation," *Nation and Ideology* (Boulder, CO: East European Monographs, 1981), pp. 463–479; and Ervand Abrahamian, "Kasravi: The Integrative Nationalist," *Middle Eastern Studies* 9 (1972): 271–295. As for a sample of Kasravi's writing in English, there is *On Islam and Shiism*, translated by M.R. Ghanoonparvar (Costa Mesa, CA: Mazdâ Publishers, 1990).

Persian for them was a local dialect, like the Persian of those who had gone to Europe and the United States during the twenty-year period before the Revolution. As a result, not only did they not have any feeling or love for Persian, but also in speaking and writing they regularly employed Arabic words and phrases as testimony to their learning and sophistication.

National Feeling and Regard for the National Language

From the dawn of the Constitutional Movement, the subject matter of Persian prose changes and its scope broadens. Writers, readers, styles of expression and prose genres all change. But the position of religious scholars on nationality underwent no change and exhibited the same views as Ghazâli and Majlesi, the same view as always. In the words of Mortazâ Motahhari:

> The issue of 'nation-worship' in the present age has created a significant problem for the world of Islam. Besides the fact that the notion of nationalism is contrary to Islamic doctrine insofar as in the view of Islam all elements are without distinction, this notion is a great barrier to the unity of Muslims . . . As followers of one religion and one set of principles and one ideology by the name of Islam, in which the element of nationality does not exist, we cannot remain indifferent with respect to antagonistic currents that take shape under the name and banner of nationality."[58]

If a relationship exists between Iranian national sentiment and interest in the national language, the level of attachment of today's religious scholars to the Persian language ought not to be greater than the respect of earlier religious scholars for this language. In the business of religion, Persian is useful for oral contact with the mass of believers, while writing in it is useful for the exposition of issues and problems and for propagation of the true faith of Twelver Shi'i Islam. Beyond this, however, the Persian language has no special function, nor did it in the past. That view of nationality and this interpretation of the application of language find their way into history as well; and judgment concerning the past becomes an indicator and explicator of the view and opinion of today. Another quotation from *Reciprocal Contributions of Islam and Iran* provides an example:

---

58. Zavâreh, *Reciprocal Contributions of Islam and Iran*, pp. 50, 52.

In the Sasanian Court, despite all of its genuine Iranian ethnicity, the Persian language was not at all promoted and encouraged. Their Iranian viziers likewise did not exhibit any attraction to the Persian language, just as the Shi'i Iranian Daylamites also did not. By contrast, in the fanatical Sunni and Turkish governmental system of the Ghaznavids, the Persian language experiences growth and ripening. Such facts indicate that factors and causes other than national and ethnic bias had a hand in the revival of the Persian language.[59]

To be sure, "national and ethnic feelings" cannot revive any language, much less a language such as Persian. But national awareness and feeling are not synonymous with "national and ethnic bias." Khorâsân, the locale for the nurturing and growth of the Persian language and its home, was also a center for Islamic studies, Traditions, Sufism and Arabic language and literature from the seventh and eighth centuries.[60] Therefore, something other than "subjective prejudice" attracted the Sasanians to the Persian language. As the saying goes, "from love to fanaticism is a thousand parasangs." Moreover, fanaticism in the propagation of "the ideology of Islam" and opposition to "nationalism . . . [which] is a great barrier to the unity of Muslims" has led this Shi'i scholar and proponent of unity of Islam to write for his Iranian and Shi'i readers that pure Iranians (Sasanians) and Shi'i monarchs (Buyids) felt no attraction to the Persian language. The growth of the Persian language is the work of fanatical Sunni Turks, people of a different race and a different faith. Therefore, dear Iranian readers, the growth of your language neither derives from your nationality nor has connections with your religion.

Of course the Ghaznavids, who implemented the cultural policies of the Sasanians, played a major role in the spread of the Persian language. The same holds true of the Saljuqs, because they arrived at a time when Persian had achieved official status and had encompassed all of Iran. But why should all of this constitute evidence against the initiating and undeniable role of the Sasanians in the genesis of the Persian language?

Historical writing usually views the past from the vantage point of issues of the present. In the midst of pressing social problems and phenomena of his own age, the historian sees the past through them

59. Ibid., p. 118.
60. See further, *Cambridge History of Iran*, Vol. 2 (1985), pp. 569, 580–81.

and from within the atmosphere in which he lives. For this reason, histories written in different periods about a more distant past have different viewpoints and interpretations. Every history has within it the personality of its writer's age. Bal'ami's *History* and *Ancient Iran* by Hasan Pirniyâ (1871–1935) do not see Sasanian Iran in a similar fashion. In their views of the period, each of them introduces not only the knowledge but also the insights of their own age. The same holds for the images and interpretations in the *History of Sistân*, Rashidoddin's *Comprehensive History*, and *Târikh-e Irân* [History of Iran] by 'Abbâs Eqbâl (1896–1955) concerning the dawn of Islam and the Arab conquest of Iran.

In this fashion every worthwhile historical work is also indirectly a "history" of the historian's age. But if the historian is so bound to an ideology that it leads him to make up his mind ahead of time about the course of history and the social fate of humanity, then his "history" becomes the exposition of his hopes and the propagandization of his desires. In this situation, not only the representation of events and the ordering of historical givens, but sometimes even the choice of words is such that they guide the reader toward the author's preconceived and desired aim. For example, in the text under discussion, in the translation of the European term "nationalism," which in Persian could be *mellatgarâ'i* or *esâlat-e melliyat*, the choice of the term *mellat-parasti* [nation-worship] is not accidental. *Mellat-parasti* brings to mind other forms of *parastesh* [worship]: *shâh-parasti* [king-worship], *bot-parasti* [idol-worship], and *gusâleh-parasti* [worship of the golden calf]. *Mellat-parasti* conjures up in the subconscious of the religious reader those other forms of *parastesh*, the king-worshipping propaganda of recent years, the idolatry of the Arabs before Islam or, for example, the idolatry of Moses' people and God's wrath.

Sufis and Persian Prose

Having concluded this discussion of the court and the clergy and their conception and interpretation of national feeling, and their role in the evolution of classical Persian prose, I now turn to the third and final focus of attention, the role of Sufi gnostics in this process—and again from the same perspective and vantage point. In other words I will not actually treat gnostic prose as prose, except for one special case and that at the very end. I shall focus rather on the sociological and psychological factors in Persian writing by gnostics. The reason should be obvious. I asked earlier why clerics paid no attention to writing in Persian and why it became common among them so late, toward the end of the Safavid era, in other words, in an era when Persian had already reached its zenith and was in a process of decline.

By contrast, the chief Sufi gnostic texts sprouted and blossomed a little after the beginning of chancellery prose. Examples include: *Sharh-e Ta'arrof* [Exposition of Self-Knowledge] by Abu Ebrâhim Mosta'mali, Hojviri's *Discovery of the Hidden*, Abu 'Ali 'Osmâni's translation of Qushayri's *Risâla* or the numerous works of 'Abdollâh Ansâri (1006–1089), all of them from the end of the tenth through the

145

eleventh centuries.[1] Not to mention the famous gnostic works of 'Attâr, 'Aynolqozât, Sohravardi, and even Avicenna (980–1037), and the *Rezâleh-ye Me'râjiyan* [Ascension Treatise] and *Savâneh* [Accidents] by Imam Ahmad Ghazâli, *Secrets of Unity* or *The Book of the Perfect Man* and such other esteemed works as the *Maqâlât-e Shams*.[2]

Of poetry, too, nothing needs to be said, for we know that gnosticism becomes the undisputed master of the broad realm of poetry. The issue here is: what accounts for the fascination of Muslim mystics with Persian prose in the face of the long-standing indifference of Muslim clerics toward the language? What are the social and cultural causes of this historic event?

The audiences of Muslim gnostics and theologians were one and the same, as were their followers and pupils, except in villages, so far as we can know. No sort of statistics or survey of information exists on the social condition of the Muslim faithful and the students of mystical masters, the followers of the religious law and of the Sufi path. On the basis of the study of history and classical literature one can only have a general sense and offer conjectures. The people of religion were everywhere, in the countryside and in the cities, whereas the Sufi base was primarily in the city and among bazaris and tradespeople and craftsmen, in the larger populated areas, on the outskirts of cities, and along the caravan routes. In other words, we meet Sufis and disciples of gnosticism less among the village population. The gnostic mentality and culture usually penetrated villages indirectly, not by means of meetings and monasteries and degrees of initiation; rather, insofar as it had found its way everywhere, it permeated the countryside as well. But the city was the locus of both ways and methods. Not only were the orthodox religious and gnostics together there, but also a great number of people had both experiences within themselves and did not believe in the separation of the orthodox religion from gnosticism.

Be that as it may, theologians and gnostics in the city shared the same audience. Both groups wanted their words to reach the ears of one community, the affluent and middle class. At least here—where

---

1. [MH] E.g., 'Abdollâh Ansâri, *Monâjât* [Prayers], translated by W.M. Thackston as *Intimate Conversations* (Albany, NY: SUNY Press, 1978).

2. [MH] Examples available in English are: Ebn-e Sinâ [Avicenna], *The Metaphysical*, translated by Parviz Morewedge (London: Routledge & Kegan Paul, 1978); Jalâloddin Rumi, *Discourses of Rumi*, translated by A.J. Arberry (London: Allen & Unwin, 1961).

verse and prose and belles-lettres were promoted and nurtured—they had one and the same audience. So, why did these two groups, the adherents of orthodox religion and of gnosticism, behave in different and even conflicting ways in relating to the same audience in terms of language, the vehicle for such relations? There is no clear and satisfactory answer to this question. The issue has not been studied. One can hazard guesses and deal with generalities that might lead somewhere. First, let us examine the period beginning in the tenth century and continuing to the Mongol period, because after that the nature of Sufism changes, as does its relationship with language.

Two Manifestations of One Religion

From the ninth and tenth centuries to the threshold of the Constitutional Movement, Iranian Islam had two characters in terms of culture. We might say that we Iranians faced two Islamic cultures. Of course, I do not mean two Islams, but two cultural forms, two intellectual manifestations of one religion in cultural life: the Islam of the *faqih*, the theologian, and the Islam of the *'âref* gnostic, the Islam of the Law and Islam of the Way. Let me state at the outset that a clear dividing line cannot be drawn between these two. A great number of gnostics were not only legalistic Muslims as well, but they also endeavored to show the oneness of these two sides of Islam and to deny their difference. Sometimes, educated clerics undertook similar efforts. Or such prominent figures as Mohammad Ghazâli were both frequenters of the mosque and denizens of the monastery. However, these two manifestations of Islam not only exhibit distinctions, but are in fundamental conflict with respect to an essential matter, the issue of knowing divine truth and hence of attaining to it.

Islam of the Law

In the view of the follower of religious law, Muslims have been given the way to attainment of divine truth. It has been presented in the Book and in the customs and Traditions of the Prophet. One must study this truth, learn it, and implement it. The way of the theologians is that of *'elm*, "scientific." We need not go into particulars. It is obvious that the sense of the term "scientific" here is religious sciences, that the concept, subject, and methods of this science differ from science in today's sense. The essence and truth of every form of knowledge appears in the Koran, e.g., 6:59, "There is not anything either green or withered but is inscribed in a clear Book." But in gnosticism (*'erfân* and *ma'refat* mean "knowing" in the sense of "familiarity" or "awareness," while *âref* denotes someone who is aware), knowing or knowledge is an intuitive matter and an interior state, and is not to be learned and consequently is not "scientific." It is something to be found, accepted, something to be discovered.

One must resort here to metaphor and say that in a twofold relation divine truth manifests itself in the mirror of the gnostic's heart. Religious law and the gnostic way both refer to a route. In the former, the rules of the road are fixed, i.e., how to behave; the customs and their regulation are fixed and one must proceed accordingly: "Go on the way as those on the way have gone." But in the latter, the way must be opened, it must reveal itself and be undertaken as it shows itself. Here an essential and significant point is that, in the Law, the curves and twists and valleys and hills of the route are known. One can therefore know the way and take others along it. One can study the "science" of knowing the way. Here the Koranic expression of "the enjoining of good and the prohibition of evil" finds its meaning. The person versed in religious law is duty bound in accordance with the regulation of the law to persuade people to do some things and to refrain from others. But in the gnostic faith, the Way or Path is an interior, personal, and private experience. It has no general and public design. It leads to the position: "Whether I am good or bad, you should go and be yourself."

The question remains as to the relevance of the above to Persian gnostic prose. There is a connection, which I shall reach in due course. For over a thousand years we have had to deal with these two aspects of Islam, these two forms, two cultural regulations of the religion. Islam of the religious law is an Islam which has an authoritarian, patriarchal and domineering character and is an indirect manifestation of tribal-rural societies. The tradition of many of its commands reaches back to the Torah. But in another sense these same commands are reminiscent of the relationship between sultan and subject, and on a higher plane the relationship of the Creator without need and the needy servant. The blessing of heaven and the tortures of hell and punishments, fasting and prayer and good works and charitable deeds, worship and ethics, venial and mortal sins from slander and thievery to adultery and blasphemy and hypocrisy, the rules of trade and contracts, war and jihâd and the spoils of war, tithing and alms, marriage and other "social functions" make up a major portion of the Koran. The theologians epitomize and represent this Islam, the Islam of religious law.

Islam of the Way

Islam has another aspect likewise manifested in the Koran in verses that are well known. It is an aspect which focuses on the relation of man with the upper world from another dimension: the "caliphate" [vice-regency] of humanity over the earth at God's behest, the burden of trusteeship which humanity accepted, the capacity to love which inheres in humans (but not in angels), the special holiness of discourse, revelation, Gabriel and the relationship of God with his prophets, i.e., with humans, and the concept of the perfect man. The number of these Koranic verses is smaller than those dealing with "social realities" and practical commands. But all of Islamic gnosticism and the Islamic gnosticism of Iran are founded on these very verses. Muslim gnostics are representative of this Islam whose characteristics differ from the Islam of the orthodox followers of the law. It is not authoritative or domineering, it has no good relations with fanaticism and rigidity of thought. On the contrary, it is easy-going and lenient.

Our discussion is not about the Sufi way or Islam of the law. Consequently, I shall content myself with this and move on. Though religious scholars (and in particular, theologians) have dealt primarily in their works with social problems affecting the community, with transactions, contracts, purification after urination and defecation, and ritual worship, gnostics have paid little attention to these matters and, in contrast, in the matter of worship they say: "Do not seek any ritual of sequence—say whatever your lonely heart wants." In the works of such gnostics as Sanâ'i, 'Attâr, Sohravardi, 'Aynolqozât and Jâmi, or in Rumi's *Masnavi*, the thrust is on the spiritual aspects of Islam. For the most part, practical commandments go unmentioned, as if they were not part of Islam. In their stead, gnostics speak of things not permissible according to the law—of love and unity, music and dancing, wine and taverns.

This Islam, the Islam of the Sufi path, has another character and sometimes even a different nature (for example, among the adherents of *vahdat-e vojud* [the unity of being] or the *malâmatis* ["reprobates"]) from the Islam of the law. This Islam (the origin of gnosticism

notwithstanding) is urban and belongs to the period of the expansion
and efflorescence of the Islamic empire. Let me briefly treat this
matter before getting to the point at issue. In the Islamic empire from
Andalusia to Transoxiana and India, in general, there was one
religion, one notion about the world and the last judgment, and even
"one" language. Arabic was the international language of the peoples
of Islam. Despite regional and national governments, borders and
wars, economic and cultural relations within the empire were
extremely active and widespread, and a dynamic commerce was
continually in operation. There was a certain professional mobility.
A North African judge sat on the judicial tribunal in Egypt; an Iranian
vizier served the caliph in Baghdad; and Turkish and Daylamite
soldiers were in the service of Arabs and non-Arabs. In this empire
divinity students and scientists, military and court personnel, judges
and tourists and, more than anything, commercial caravans constantly
came and went. Large cities were centers of commercial, scientific
and religious barter and exchange, administrative and court centers,
military bases, and sometimes all of these. In the period of growth
and splendor of Islamic civilization some cities achieved unprecedented population growth, wealth, and economic and cultural vitality;
such were Baghdad, Nishâpur, Rayy, Basra, Marv, Samarqand,
Bokhara, Damascus and Cairo.

In such cities were all kinds of people living next to and in contact
with one another: Jews, Zoroastrians, Christians, Sunnis and Shi'is
and the numerous and various sects of both major branches of Islam,
gnostics and Sufis of various hues and pedigrees, and presumably
Manichaeans, Carmathians, foreigners, and God knows what others.
Even in the small and ancient mosque at Zavâreh, a far-flung village
in the middle of a salt desert, four *mehrâb*s were situated next to one
another, presumably for prayers of the four Sunni sects.

In such cities not only did all sorts of people live, but all sorts of
people came and went. Frequently caravans and merchants who set
out with their goods on the caravans were of other peoples, languages,
religions and sects. They were obliged to spend the night in caravan-
serais and public or private lodgings and to deal with buyers and
sellers. All of this was impossible without physical, religious, and
financial security. Nothing would ever be accomplished if one's wealth
were stolen, if one could not practice one's religion, if people were
not ready to sit and eat with one another, if everything one touched
had to be washed, or if the ground where one trod had to have dirt

thrown on it, as in the time of Shâh Tahmâsp, in order to cleanse it of the pollution of an unbeliever. All of the transactions and business of God's creatures would cease. Then not only would the door of the empire have to close, but the people of the different Islamic sects would have to be segregated.

One day when a Mamluk sultan was presiding over the court of justice in Cairo, several Iranian merchants came seeking justice and said: "We have become homeless because of the oppression of the Mongols. Now in Cairo as well, people have bought from us, but instead of paying, they have wasted our wealth. The Hanafi judge has pronounced imprisoned customers insolvent, so we are left with empty pockets." The Mamluk sultan ordered the debtors out of prison and "persuaded" them to pay up. He reprimanded the Hanafi judge for his conduct and took from him the right to adjudicate such matters.[3] The point to this anecdotal digression is that, if Cairo was a city where commerce should take place and if the Sultan wanted to assure a flourishing economic life for his capital, laws and customs had to exist there that were the same for everyone, at least in the realm of commerce and trade, regardless of nationality, language, religion or sect.

Differences of opinion and religious and sectarian conflicts naturally existed in Islamic cities as a matter of course. Sometimes they led to violence and even death or conflagrations. Maqdisi, Yâqut, Ibn Battutah, Khwândamir, and others have reported such events. But in general in the period of splendor of Islamic civilization, city-dwellers coexisted for the most part in an environment of toleration and lack of bias. In order to get on with their own lives, residents of these cities, sites of the proverbial "seventy-two sects," were obliged to forgo warring with many of these "sects."[4]

Gnostic Islam is the Islam of such cities. It is urban Islam to which the exigencies of civil life lent another character, encouraging leniency and tolerance toward others and a sense of fellowship. Gnostics represent and manifest this Islam. As a matter of fact, Sufis of the ninth, tenth, and eleventh centuries belonged mostly to the cities of Greater

---

3. David Ayalon, "The Great Yâsa of Chingiz Khan, a re-examination," *Studia Islamica* 38 (1973), p. 115.

4. A different, though related, phenomenon is tackled in Hosayn Mirja'fari, "The Haydari-Ni'mati Conflicts in Iran," translated by J.R. Perry, *Iranian Studies* 12 (1978): 135–162.

Khorâsân or the villages adjacent to these cities, to a region which was one of the first centers of Muslim civilization and culture in Iran.

Mystic and Scholar and the Government Apparatus

Let me now pose this question in a different form: What characteristics of the Islamic gnosticism of Iran led it to adopt the Persian language, whereas theologians and jurisprudents did not? Whence the difference in role of these two manifestations of one phenomenon?

First is the fact that Sufism had nothing to do with the caliphate and government, and even knowingly and deliberately turned its back on them. This is an effect and consequence of the philosophy and experience of Sufism. In contrast, the religious scholar, and especially the theologian, did business with the institutions of government because of their religious and social responsibilities, because of judicial matters, religious endowments, financial matters of the mosques, schools, and religious establishments and organizations, and in order to implement many legal matters and edicts. In turn, the governments also needed religious scholars and theologians. Consequently, religious and governmental organizations, organizations dealing with the next world and with this world, were mutually dependent and interdependent. Of course some pious theologians always kept their distance from government; but the religious institution as a whole was not without links to it.

This difference made the Sufi independent of the official language of government, i.e., Arabic, at least to the extent that it concerned relations between national and local governments of Iran and the Baghdad caliphate. In contrast, the religious scholar and theologian were not free of that political connection and its language; they had business with it, and in some instances they themselves even served as intermediaries in the relationship.

More important than this, as a result of his relationship with the government establishment that derives from his religious position, the theologian enjoys advantages such as are not at the Sufi's disposal, or at least not to the same extent. Earlier I mentioned the theologian's "oral means": the mosque and the pulpit and all of the means of group communication of the age, in addition to the administrative facilities of the court and the financial possibilities of the religious foundations, votive gifts, etc. Here there is little difference between Sunni and Shi'i.

When Sunnism was the official religion, the Shiites and their theologians were free within their own regions; in such cities as Qom, Sabzavâr, Rayy, Kâshân and Sâri they were almost always in the majority. In any case, despite the considerable influence of Islam, and even though the Sufi sometimes had access to the mosque and pulpit, he never had at his disposal all of these possibilities for contact with followers. The Sufi has limitations in this respect.

At the risk of oversimplification and without further delving into the subject, one can say that because oral means of communication, which were the most general and effective, were not readily available to Sufis, Sufis naturally chose written speech to contact people and deliver their own message, writing in the language of the audience, that is to say, Persian. This consideration perhaps accounts for some of the facts. Now let us take a look at this same fact, the link between Sufism and the Persian language, from another perspective.

We know the relationship between Sufism and science. I have already stated that mystical knowledge (and the attainment of the creative truth which is its aim) does not derive from science. In the Sufi view, science is the domain of talkers, not people who experience spiritual states; science belongs to a handful of foolish power seekers. Of course, healthy Sufism—not the affectation of dervish behavior in periods of decline—is not opposed to acquired science. A great number of our leading Sufis were Catholic in their day's cultural affairs. But they despised the snobbery of science, and people who used it as a refuge and deemed it the source of salvation; they considered it the stuff of self-aggrandizement and inadequacy. They maintained one had to put this stage behind one and free oneself of lessons and ledgers. Although they did not approve of illiterate clerics, they did not consider expertise in theology a condition for being a full human being. Consequently, the Sufi as scholar refused to countenance his own scholarship and berated himself for it. In the case of the language of science (Arabic), the situation was the same. Even when the Sufi knew it well, he did not insist on displaying his knowledge or writing in Arabic, except when dealing with the Koran.

A Language Other than the Language of Science

While the Sufi kept his distance from science and the language of science, his turning to Persian was linked with the language as a source of rapture and loss of self, a change of state. This is exactly what

scholars and theologians abhorred, because this preparation led the
believer to a state and an arena which were outside the jurisdiction of
the legalists, and one path they did not consider permissible. The
theologian was essentially opposed to the use of language for such a
purpose. The following story from *Asrâr al-Towhid* [Secrets of Divine
Unity] by Mohammad Ebn-e Monavvar (fl. 1157–1202) reveals both
the cause of this opposition and the reason for the Sufi use of Persian:

> A story: Khâjeh Hasan Mo'addeb who was the special servant of
> Shaykh Abu Sa'id [ibn Abi'l-Khayr, d. 1048], recounted that, when
> at the beginning of his career Abu Sa'id came to Nishâpur and held
> meetings, people immediately turned to him, and many became his
> followers. In Nishâpur at that time the leader of the Karramiyya sect
> was Master Abu Bakr Es'hâq Karrâmi, and the chief magistrate was
> Qâzi Sâ'ed. Both of them had many followers, and they completely
> rejected the Shaykh, and considered all Sufis enemies.
>
> And the Shaykh was reciting verses from the pulpit and was inviting
> people to feasts, such that he spent more than one thousand *dinâr*s
> on one feast, and he continually sang. And they made vociferous
> objections, and the Karrâmi imams and the magistrates signed a
> deposition that a man from Mihaneh had come into their midst and
> was holding meetings and proselytizing for Sufism and that he
> recited poetry from the pulpit. Instead of Koranic commentary and
> Prophetic Traditions, he was singing songs [*samâ'*] and dancing and
> inciting the young men to dance. Moreover, he was eating almond
> cake, colored fruit, and roast chicken. He calls himself an ascetic,
> and says that his verses are ascetic verses, Sufi verse! The people
> have flocked to him and have lost their way. The bulk of the
> population are on the verge of rioting. If something is not done
> about this situation, a riot will soon break out. They sent the
> deposition to Ghaznayn, to the Ghaznavid Sultan. On the back of
> the message came the answer, that both the Shâfi'ite and Hanifite
> legalists should convene to investigate this situation and force upon
> Abu Sa'id what religious law [*shari'at*] requires. The response
> arrived on Thursday. Those opposed to Abu Sa'id rejoiced and said,
> Tomorrow is Friday, so on Saturday we will announce a public
> meeting and hang this shaykh and all other Sufis at the crossroads.[5]

Elsewhere in the same book, the author writes: "The Shaykh used
to recite verses and poems in his talks. He would invite people to

5. Mohammad Ebn-e Monavvar, *Asrâr al-Towhid fi Maqâmât al-Shaykh Abi Sa'id*
[Secrets of Unity in the Stages of Shaykh Abu Sa'id], edited by Zabihollâh Safa
(Tehran: Amir Kabir, 1975, 3rd printing, first published in 1953), p. 77.

feasts. People would continually sing and dance around him. For this reason, the leaders of all sects rejected him."[6]

As Abu Sa'id put it in these typical couplets which he recited from the pulpit and which elicited the wrath of religious scholars:

> I see all of your beauty when I open my eyes,
> My whole body becomes a heart when I confide in you.
> I hold it forbidden to talk with others;
> When I tell my secrets to you, I speak at length.[7]

Sufism is a religion or, better said, a religious way, different from the dominant religion of those who follow religious law. It is a knowledge that is different from and often in opposition to acquired knowledge, whether religious or otherwise . . . This different phenomenon turned to a language other than the official language of religion and science to express the state and narratives of its own soul, the language of gnostic disciples. In the preface to *Tazkerat al-owliyâ* [Lives of the Saints], 'Attâr (d.c. 1230) says, concerning the reasons for compiling biographies of Sufis: "Another reason was that because the Koran and Prophetic Traditions and narratives require a knowledge of the vocabulary and grammar and syntax [of Arabic] and the majority of people are not capable of deriving benefit from the content of such works, these words which are explanations of those works and which people high and low can benefit from, although the original works are in Arabic, I have turned them into Persian so that all be included."[8]

Here two points deserve to be noted. One is 'Attâr's view of lives and speech of Sufis as tantamount to an explanation of the Koran and Prophetic Traditions. Second is the use of Persian instead of Arabic so that everyone might take advantage of Sufi talk and writing. These "people high and low" were primarily tradesmen, bazaar merchants, and middle-class city people, but also members of the nobility and the wealthy, who in circles and meetings, in gatherings and at monastic establishments, expected their elders and guides to explain the symbolism of love, the mysteries of union and the stages of the mystical journey. For followers of religious law, the Koran and Prophetic Tradi-

6. Ibid., p. 145.
7. Abu Sa'id ibn Abi al-Khayr, *Hâlât va Sokhanân-e Abu Sa'id* [Abu Sa'id's States and Statements], edited by Iraj Afshâr (Tehran: 1970), p. 34.
8. [MH] Faridoddin 'Attâr, *Tazkerat al-awliyâ* [Lives of the Saints]; translated by A.J. Arberry as *Muslim Saints and Mystics* (University of Chicago Press, 1966).

tions sufficed. But followers of the Sufi way wanted something else besides that, and that in their own language.

Persian, the Language of Sufi Devotees

Just as Prophetic Traditions represented a parable of the Koran in written form, so too the followers of the Sufi path wanted, besides those writings, lasting mementos of their own way and method, which Iranian Sufism—except for a brief initial period—created by means of the Persian language.

"The reason for the writing of the *Masnavi* in Persian was that when Chelebi Hosâmoddin discovered his friends' attraction to 'Attâr's *Elâhinâmeh* [Book of Divinity] and his *Mosibatnâmeh* [Book of Afflictions], he made a request of Mowlâ(nâ) to the effect that there was plenty of gnostic lore in *ghazal*s, and if a book were to be composed in couplets, along the lines of the *Elâhinâmeh* of Sanâ'i (d. 1140) or 'Attâr's *Manteq al-Tayr* [Conference of the Birds] so that his friends might have a lasting memento, that would be the greatest favor."[9]

More expressive than others are the words of Najmoddin Râzi (d. 1256) in his famous book called *Mersâd al-'ebâd* [Watchtower of God's Servants] (1221–1223), where he discusses the reason for writing the book, particularly in Persian:

> [Quoting the Koran, in Arabic] Almighty God said, We have sent no prophet except in the language of his people to explain to them, and the Prophet, peace be upon him, said [quoting Hadith in Arabic], Talk to people according to the extent of their understanding. Know [in Persian] that though many long and short books have been written on the Sufi Path, they are mostly in Arabic and are not very useful to Persian speakers.
>
> One must tell an old sorrow to a new beloved,
> One must speak to her in her language.
> "Fais-le" and "ne fais-le pas" are not of much use;
> When you are with a Persian you must say 'do it' and "don't do it."

9. 'Abdorrahman Jâmi, *Nafahât al-uns*, edited by M. Towhidipur (Tehran: Ketâbforushi-ye Sa'di, 1958), p. 468. [MH], On Sanâ'i, see J.T.P. deBruijn, *Of Piety and Poetry: The Interaction of Religion and Literature in the Life and Works of Hakim Sana'i of Ghazna* (Leiden: E.J. Brill, 1983). On 'Attâr, see *The Conference of the Birds*, translated by Afkham Darbandi and Dick Davis (Harmondsworth, Middlesex: Penguin Books, 1984).

For some time a group of scholarly seekers and sincere disciples have been requesting of yours truly . . . a compendium in Persian, short but full of meaning which would tell of the beginning and end of creation and the start and end of the mystical journey and the aim and goal of lover and beloved. It should be both a world-displaying cup and a beauty-reflecting mirror. It should be useful to both the imperfect beginner and the person nearing perfection.[10]

So, Râzi's rationale for writing in Persian is to speak in the language of friends. If it were not for the desire and requests of these friends, the book would not have been written. In other words, as in the case of many of the works of the Sufis, just as writing is the result of the desire of the writer, it is likewise the product of disciples' wishes. Sayyid Haydar Âmoli, the famous Shi'i Sufi of the fourteenth century who wrote in both Arabic and Persian, says that just as the divine word was revealed in Hebrew, Syriac, Arabic, and the like, the difference in expressing things in Arabic or Persian, Hindi or Greek, does not bring about a difference in the meaning of the original.[11] Thus Âmoli wrote his books in Persian or Arabic in accordance with the wishes of friends and depending upon their knowledge of the language. Most of the treatises in *Ketâb-e Ensân-e Kâmel* [Book of the Perfect Man], the work of the famous Sufi 'Azizoddin Nasafi, as is stated in the preface, were prepared "at the request of a community of dervishes."[12]

In the Safavid period, despite the fact that Turkish also entered the fray with Arabic, the language of the Sufis remained Persian as it had been in the past. In his *History of Literature in Iran*, Safâ cites a number of Safavid era commentaries and books. The vast majority are in Persian, with only a few in Turkish and Arabic.[13]

---

10. 'Abdollâh b. Mohammad Najmoddin Râzi, *Mersâd al-'ebâd min al-mabda' ila al-mi'âd*, edited by Mohammad Amin Riyâhi (Tehran: Bongâh-e Tarjomeh va Nashr-e Ketâb, 1973), p. 14.

11. Shaykh Sayyid Haydar Âmoli, *Jâme' al-Asrâr wa Manba' al-Anvâr* [Compendium of Secrets and Source of Lights], with notes by Henri Corbin and Osmân Yahyâ (Tehran: Franco-Iranian Institute, 1969), pp. 613ff.

12. 'Azizoddin Mohammad Nasafi, *Majmu'eh-ye rasâ'el mashhur be-Ketâb al-ensân al-kâmel* [Compendium of Treatises Known as the Book of the Perfect Man], edited and introduced (in French) by Marian Molé (Tehran: Franco-Iranian Institute, 1980, first printed in 1962).

13. Safa, "Âsâr-e Sufiyân" [Works of the Sufis], *History of Literature in Iran*, vol. 5, part 1.

In addition to the above, let me present an example from a later period, from a time when Sufism had given up its active and productive social and cultural role, from Sufism's period of decline during which, however, the same attachment to the Persian language persists. It is a quotation from Safi 'Ali Shâh's own autobiography:

> The birthplace of your humble servant was Isfahan, where I was born in November 1835. My father was a merchant who went from Isfahan to Yazd and chose to live there. I was a small child at that time. I remained in Yazd for twenty years. Afterwards I traveled to the Hejâz by way of India, and I met with most of the elders of Iran and India and Turkey. From some of them I derived some slight benefit, and I learned the rules of poverty and the Way, the acquisition of which is exclusively a matter of serving and accepting the divine will, by adherence to a particular gnostic tradition, the description of which is lengthy and will not fit into this brief discussion. In India I succeeded in writing *Zobdat al-Asrâr* [Cream of Secrets], in verse which treats martyrdom and conformity to the Way toward God. Setting out via the holy earth of Imam Rezâ [Mashhad] and the lofty shrines [Najaf und Karbala], I returned to Shiraz and Yazd. And I came to Tehran because residing at the Dâr ol-Khelâfa [capital city] is more secure for everyone, in particular the likes of us people from other regions, especially in this period when the Sultan of the Sultans of the Age, may God perpetuate his kingdom and his government, is the king of Iran . . . and where the majority of the people have acquired learning and skill, and have adopted decent conduct. I also stayed in this kingdom and I have now resided in tranquility for over twenty years in the capital. And I am not at odds in discourse or station with anyone. And if I have seen some intemperate deeds done by either the idle or the active, and if I have heard some jaundiced talk, I have put up with it . . . most of my time is spent in writing. In these several years I have written a treatise, *'Erfân al-haqq* [Knowledge of God] and also *Bahr al-haqâ'eq* [Sea of Truths] and *Mizân al-ma'refeh* [The Scales of Knowledge]. For nearly two years I have been busy compiling a Koranic commentary in verse which is both something for me to do and a work of devotion and also an encouragement to Persian-speaking people to read and understand the noble word of God. Perhaps the recompense of your humble servant's merit will not be lost on God.[14]

---

14. Safi 'Ali Shâh, *Tafsir-e Qor'ân* [Commentary on the Koran] (Tehran: Khayyâm, 1963), *Sharh-e ahvâl . . . be-qalam-e khodash* [Autobiography of S. 'A.].

Several points deserve emphasis. The writer is urban and from a merchant family. Like the majority of Sufis, he travels far and wide, and he seeks a shaykh and a group. Not every city is safe for Sufis (not to speak of villages); or, the capital is a safer place. This shaykh is a writer of Persian and, like many Sufis, is a devotee of poetry. He sees no conflict between the way of religious Law and the Sufi Way (*Zobdat al-asrâr*). But another particularly significant point is that his Koranic commentary is in verse, while the Koran itself is not sympathetic to poetry, which theologians reject. The reason for writing in Persian is the perennial one: the enjoyment and benefit of those who do not know Arabic, getting "the message" across and establishing communication with Persian-speaking people and, more important, with Persian-speaking disciples.

The Language of Rapture and Mystical States

Persian writing by Sufis has another basic cause as well. Mysticism is an internal experience and a spiritual state which are difficult to describe. Mystics have always argued that all means and modes for the description of the mystic's internal experience are inexpressive and ineloquent, especially the dry language of science, the language of formal discourse. In the words of a friend, mysticism seeks a language expressive of states, an internal language which wells up from the depths of the soul, that is to say, one's mother tongue, not a language that one later learns and that comes into one from the outside, regardless of how well it permeates one's mind and there reigns. If this view is correct, it is therefore natural that Iranian Sufism opens its mouth in Persian, not for exposition of realities which reason comprehends, but rather for the revelation of truth disclosed to the soul.

In *Kashf al-asrâr wa mukâshafat al-anwâr* [Disclosing of Secrets and Revelation of Lights], which is the description of his mystical dreams and spiritual experiences, Ruzbehân Baqli of Shiraz (c. 1123–1209) says that he saw "God on the porch of his house, that the whole world appeared like a shining light, overflowing and mighty. Then from within this light, He called my name seven times and said in Persian: 'O Ruzbehân, I have chosen you in friendship!' "[15] Despite the fact that Ruzbehân wrote *Disclosing of Secrets* in Arabic, God's words to him and his language of secrets and the discourse of his innermost soul is Persian.

---

15. Henri Corbin, *En Islam Iranien*, vol. 3, p. 45.

In *Lives of the Saints*, 'Attâr says: "After the Koran and Prophetic Traditions, no speech is nobler than the speech of Sufi shaykhs, because their words are the result of experience and mystical states, not the fruits of memory and formal discourse . . . these shaykhs are heirs to the prophets." When adherents of the Sufi way, who always belittled the memorization and discourse of religious scholars, wander in the "green gardens of love" and in a state in which "not one of their veins is sober," how could they explain the transformation of their existence and the selflessness of their soul with discourse which at least for them is the product of memorization and rhetoric, which began with [the Arabic grammatical paradigm] "Zayd struck 'Amr," which passed through the twists and turns of grammar and syntax and the words which they learned formally one by one until they mastered it? Moreover, the majority of followers of the Sufi way do not know Arabic. A more precise and conclusive treatment of this subject would result from scrutiny of the writings of our bilingual Sufis to discern what subjects they have written about in Arabic and what matters they have treated in their mother tongue. Is there a difference between the subjects or not? Can one classify them and see a specific logic at work or not? I leave answers to the experts.

Moreover, such Sufi works as Rumi's *Divân-e Shams* [Collected Poems Dedicated to Shams of Tabriz] and *Masnavi*, Ruzbehân's *Sharh-e Shathiyât* [Exposition of Ecstatic Utterances], Nasafi's *Book of the Perfect Man* or the treatises of 'Aynolqozât were written at the request and wishes of friends, disciples, and dervishes, and even with their physical or spiritual collaboration. These works are not the results of solitary reflections of their poets and writers. The result is a sort of spiritual collaboration, a linking corresponding to the Sufi state and a sympathy and harmony of like-minded people of an assembly or monastery, in short, fellow-travelers along the Sufi path. Although these works are deeply personal, persons other than their authors are also not without influence in their creation. Others have a role in them. The means of verification of this deep inner experience, the path to their achieving the state and soul of one another, is naturally the mother tongue, Persian, and not any other language. In the words of 'Abdolhosayn Zarrinkub, "Among the Sufis were persons more affected by poetry and music than by the Koran, such that Yusof b. al-Hasan Râzi used to be moved to tears by poetry recited with emotion and spirit, but did not reach this state with the Koran."[16]

Interest in National Myths and Narratives

In contrast to religious scholars, the Sufis did not reject and repudiate fables and the national epic of ancient Iran or consider them idle Magian tales, a threat to one's faith, unworthy of approval or even outright heretical. In fact, Sufis displayed interest in them. One of the cornerstones of Sohravardi's Illuminationist philosophy was "Khos-ravâni" [*khosrow*=king] wisdom, the thought and wisdom of pre-Islamic Iran. Sohravardi's Persian treatises are full of "philosophical-gnostic" reconstruction and interpretation of Iranian myths and legends, like references in 'Aynolqozât's writing to Rakhsh, Rostam, Zâl, Shabdiz, Khosravâni aspirations, and other things. We see interest in the myth of the birds and the Simurgh, the freedom of the soul and the cage of the body not only in Sohravardi, but also in writings from Avicenna (980–1037) to Nasiroddin Tusi (1201–1274)—so far as their mystical ideas are concerned—and others, a myth that reaches its culmination in 'Attâr's *Conference of the Birds*. We know that Jâmi (1414–1492) and other Sufis as well did not limit themselves to Koranic stories, but also employed our own ancient myths and legends.

In addition, we know that *fotovvat* [chivalry] was related to gnosticism and Sufism. In fact, *fotovvat* was a sort of vernacular gnosticism and Sufism of craftsmen and bazaris. Ancient myths and folktales such as *Samak-e ayyâr* [Samak the Rogue], *Hamza-nâmeh* [The Story of Hamzeh], *Dârâb-nâmeh* [The Book of Dârâb], *Sandabâd-nâmeh* [The Book of Sandabâd], and Shabestari's *Hosayn Kord* [Hosayn the Kurd] became popular through professional storytellers and raconteurs among middle-class city people and constituted a major portion of their culture.[17] Even greater was the interest taken in the heroes of epic and *shâhnâmeh* legends and the stories born of them, as in the scrolls of oral storytellers.

---

16. 'Abdolhosayn Zarrinkub, *Arzesh-e mirâs-e sufiyyeh* [Value of the Legacy of Su-fism] (Tehran: Amir Kabir, 1974), p. 95.

17. [MH] The most readily available English version of such medieval Persian prose romances is *Love and War, Adventures from the Firuz Shâh Nâma of Sheikh Bighami*, translated and introduced by William L. Hanaway, Jr. (Delmar, NY: Scholars' Facsimiles & Reprints, 1974).

The point to the citation of these examples is that the conceptual-ization, plotting, redaction, and interpretation of legends or Iranian epics and myths by means of Sufism or currents related to it (for instance, *fotovvat*) inevitably created a kinship and affinity of thought with the language of these legends and stories (or the language in which the substance of them had remained and which gave them continued life), that is, the Persian language. Legends and language interact like twins and companions in the totality of a culture. The writer or speaker who "lives" a legend breathes in the atmosphere of its language. Perhaps this is another reason for the devotion of our Sufi mystics to the Persian language.

The Change in the Social Role of Sufism

From the thirteenth and fourteenth centuries, that is, during the Mongol and later the Timurid ages, the social situation of Sufism in Iran changed. From a spiritual organization based on sensual experi-ence, it turned into a powerful social organization, with institutions and property and endowed foundations in communication with the authorities and rulers, the bands of disciples and monastery dwellers hired and mobilized to participate in local disputes and conflicts. Various factors contributed to this transformation. We know that the Mongols did not have a "proper" religion and for some time did not exercise any bias or fanaticism in being Muslim, in contrast, for example, with the early Turkish Ghaznavids and Saljuqs who were more Catholic than the Pope, as it were. As the well-known story about Sultan Mahmud of Ghazna puts it, he searched everywhere for Carmathians to send to the gallows.

From the thirteenth century, hives of unofficial Islam, both Shi'i and Sufi, gathered strength. Tamerlane also, who beat his breast in tune with Islamic fanaticism—evidently under the influence of the shamanism of the Central Asian Turks—displayed a weakness for the dervishhood and pseudo-Sufism of members of monastic estab-lishments who claimed to have secret lore and miraculous powers. Tamerlane was bloodthirsty and merciless and at the same time super-stitious. Likewise, perhaps out of political considerations (although where his sword achieved results he was not the contemplative type), he was sympathetic to shaykhs and religious scholars.

Moreover, the domination of the Mongols and the Timurids led the people to despair of society and to adopt pseudo-Sufism (not mysticism) and boosted the market for this. In any case, whatever the causes, it is true that in this period, on account of the gullibility and simplicity of the people at large, the fake asceticism, hypocrisy, and spiritual profiteering enjoyed considerable success, both among Sufis and among religious scholars. Each group carried out its business with much pomp and circumstance and did not stay on the sidelines of the business of the government and nation. We see signs of these religious scholars and Sufis, "this handful of vain position-seekers" in *mush o gorbeh* [Mouse and Cat] and other works of 'Obayd Zakâni (d. 1371)[18] and in Hafez's poem in which the judge, mufti, jurisprudent, and municipal constable are of the same cloth and ilk.

A couple of examples would be appropriate here. The wealth and power and extent of material and spiritual influence of Shah Ne'matollâh Vali (d. 1431) were such that presents sent to him equaled the taxes of a country in value. Yet the ruler of Kermân was afraid to request taxes on such gifts from Shah Ne'matollâh, who had contact and association with rulers and leaders of his day from Shiraz and Kermân to Khorâsân and Samarqand.[19] The military expeditions and monarchical claims of Shaykh Jonayd and other ancestors of the Safavid dynasty are another example.

Essentially it is from this period that the word "shah" is added before the name of Sufis with fame, wealth or position. The children and descendants of Shah Ne'matollâh Vali had the following names: Shah Khalilollâh, Shah Nurollâh, Shah Shamsoddin Mohammad, Shah Mohebboddin Habibollâh, Shah Habiboddin Mohebbollâh, Shah Khalilollâh the Second, Shah Ne'matollâh the Second, and Amir [Prince] Nâzemoddin 'Abdolbâqi.[20] Mas'ud Homâyuni lists twenty-nine "shahs" of the Ne'matollâhi clan in Iran and twelve "shahs" of the clan in India[21] by virtue of whose existence, Iran and India were

18. [MH] 'Obayd Zakâni, *Mush o Gorbeh* [Mouse and Cat], with caricatures by Parviz Shâpur (Tehran: Morvârid, 2535/1977), translated by Omar Pound as *Gorby and the Rats* (Fayetteville, AR: The University of Arkansas Press, 1989).

19. Javâd Nurbakhsh Kermâni, *Zendegi va Âsâr-e Jenâb-e Shâh Ne'matollâh Vali* [Life and Works of Shah Ne'matollâh Vali] (Tehran: Musavi, 1958/9), p. 38.

20. Ibid., pp. 99–112.

21. Mas'ud Homâyuni, *Târikh-e Selseleh'ha-ye Tariqeh-ye Ne'matollâhiyeh dar Irân* [History of the Ne'matollâhi Lineages in Iran], second edition (Tehran: Maktab-e 'Erfân-e Iran, 1979, 2nd printing), pp. 29–31.

"shahestâns" [lands of kings]. Alongside the endless shahs, only one—"Amir" [prince] Nâzemoddin 'Abd ol-Bâqi—was dervishly modest enough to content himself with being a prince.

During this period, cultural life does not wither away, but rather we meet great names in the world of scholarship, art, literary culture and gnosticism, and outstanding works are produced. Architecture, and especially painting, reach new or higher plateaus. Nasiroddin Tusi and Qotboddin Shirâzi are two leading names of the period, while Jalâloddin Rumi, Sa'di, and Hafez have their own special places. It is still too soon for that lethal blow of the Mongols to do away with everything of ours. In Sufi prose, too, some of the most important works are being written. Bahâ'oddin Valad's *Ma'âref* [Gnostics] and the famous book by Ezzoddin Mahmud Kâshâni called *Mesbâh al-hedâya* [Lamp of Guidance] are among this period's writings, which continue up to the works of such as Jâmi in *Nafahât al-ons* [Breaths of Familiarity] and *Lavâyeh* [Flashes]. The style of these writings does not embody the simplicity, intensity of emotion and beauty of the works of earlier Sufis. But despite a little floridity, the language has remained healthy and whole and not jumbled.

With the works and teachings of Ibn 'Arabi (1165–1240), theoretical Sufism achieved its apogee and its ultimate expansion and perfection. The school of Ibn 'Arabi, particularly in Iran, attracted attention and interest to the point that such leading figures as Rumi and Jâmi turned to it. Iranians authored most of the commentaries on Ibn 'Arabi's numerous works, whether in Arabic or Persian. From this period, Sufi gnosticism itself became a sort of science, while its language became full of technical and scientific expressions, thus losing that fluidity and beauty of its earlier prose. The literary value of mystical language relinquished its place to other cultural values, among them the psychological, intellectual and philosophical, and sociological.

The Affinity of Shiism and Sufism

As Shiism spread in the sixteenth and seventeenth centuries, Sufism and Shiism drew close to one another. As we know, the Safavids based their mission and rule on the twin foundations of Shiism and Sufism. In this period some shaykhs and dynasties are either already Shi'i as in the case of the Nurbakhsh order, or, as in the case of Shah Ne'matollâh and Shaykh Shafioddin, later became Shi'i. In addition, according to Sayyid Hosayn Nasr, such sixteenth-century "Shi'i Sufis [as] Sa'doddin

Hamaviyeh, 'Abdorrazzâq Kâshâni, Ibn Torkeh, Sayyid Haydar 'Âmoli, and Ibn Abi Jomhur were completely under the influence of the teachings of Ibn 'Arabi. Moreover, Shi'i philosophers whose ideas reach their culmination in the school of Mollâ Sadrâ also need to be mentioned."[22]

From the very beginning, numerous ideological affinities existed between Sufism and Shiism. Although the early Sufis and their dynastic brotherhoods were Sunni, nevertheless nearly all of them traced their Sufi robes back to the Prophet Mohammad's son-in-law 'Ali (d. 661), the first Shi'i Imam.[23] In fact, the early Sufis were the spiritual offspring of the family of the Prophet. In the case of such leaders as Abu Yazid (d. 874) or Abu Sa'id (d. 1048), some of their later followers traced their ancestry back to the Prophet. These two were henceforth both physical and spiritual heirs. Blessed on both sides, the view that believers in the Sufi path have of a shaykh is similar to the Shi'i notion of the Imam. Both are perfect human beings and are to be obeyed. The perfection of both has a divine origin, which is hereditary for one but not for the other. In any case, without this link to God, one cannot attain salvation. There are many other similarities in the concepts, interpretations and paths of spiritual and supernatural experience.[24]

The Conflict Between Jurisprudent and Sufi

The affinity of Sufism and Shiism, however, is not at all grounds for resolution of conflict. Sufis of this period are Shi'is, as are most of the people, particularly from the Safavid period onward. But Shi'i theologians continue to reject Sufism and its spiritual and sensual experience and consider it error and apostasy. According to this view, the religious law has shown the straight and narrow path in all matters of this world and the next; traveling by another way can mean nothing other than losing one's way. I have already presented Majlesi's view. In no period did religious scholars accept Sufi views, just as they gave no approval

---

22. Sayyid Hosayn Nasr, *Le Shiism imamite* (Paris: Presses universitaires de France), p. 208.

23. Apparently only the Naqshbandis trace their *kherqeh* ["ragged robe," the symbol of initiation and succession] back to Abu Bakr, but even that is through the Shi'i Imam Ja'far Sâdeq (d. 765).

24. A subject Henri Corbin studied more than anyone else, especially in *En Islam Iranien*.

to the Isfahan school of Shi'i philosopher, Mollâ Sadrâ and others. Constant strife and discord between theologian and Sufi continued throughout the Safavid and Qajar periods down to the beginning of the Constitutional Movement. Today, too, this conflict persists, albeit no gnostics remain to face the opposition.

For further clarification, let me cite the views of two other religious scholars concerning Sufis. In the words of the Safavid scholar Moqaddas Ardabili:

> Some of the philosophers, like Ibn 'Arabi and Shaykh 'Aziz Nasafi and 'Abdorrazzâq Kâshâni have propagated unbelief and heresy, believe in the Unity of Existence [*wahdat al-wujûd*] and claim that every extant thing is God. Almighty is God, far beyond what heretics claim. One should know also that the cause for their stubborn sedition was that they busied themselves in the study of books by [Greek] philosophers, and when they had gleaned information from the words of Plato and his followers, out of grossest error they adopted the enormities of his slogans, and in order to disguise their plagiarism of the heinous essays and ideas of philosophers, dressed them in another guise and called the result "Unity of Being."[25]

This was the view of notable religious scholars of the Safavid era. Now hear what Mohammad Karim Khan Kermâni, the famous Shaykhi leader of the Qajar era, has to say about Sufism. He wishes that God "damn them and make them suffer his multifarious torments, because they have misled the people and diverted them from the path of gnosis."[26]

The Decline of Sufism

In the Safavid and Qajar eras, cultural and ethical decline reared its unholy head. As a cultural and deeply ethical phenomenon, Sufism underwent a double decline. The authentic intellectual and experimental tradition of thought and experience of Sufism continued its life from Mollâ Sadrâ to Haj Mollâ Hâdi Sabzavâri and Aqâ Mohammad

---

25. Ahmad b. Mohammad Azerbaijani, known as Moqaddas-e Ardabili, *Hadiqat al-Shi'a* [Garden of Shiism] (Tehran: Shams; Qom: Hekmat), p. 566. [MH] For Ibn [al-] Arabi in English, there is *Sufis of Andalusia: The Rûh al-quds and al-Durrat al-fâkhirah*, translated by R.W.J. Austin (London: Allen & Unwin, 1971).

26. Haj Mohammad Karim Khan Kermâni, *Ershâd al-'avâmm* [Guidance of the Masses], (Kerman: Sa'âdat, fourth printing), p. 25.

Rezâ Qomeshah'i among philosophers, but in isolation and away from society, enmeshed with philosophy and especially with Illuminationist philosophy, in the two languages Arabic and Persian. These philosophers, divorced from social life, preserved gnostic thought in their small groups and infrequent gatherings, a subject beyond the scope of our discussion. But the "gnosticism" present in the cultural and practical life of society underwent transformation into a sort of pseudo-Sufism and dervishhood which became mixed and confused, especially in the Qajar age, with mendicancy, geomancy, arithmomancy, exorcism and spirit conjuring, the claims of occult sciences, self-mortification and eventually freeloading and begging.

Interestingly, in this period and even from the days of Shâh Ne'matollâh Vali (d. 1431) and Shaykh Safioddin Ardabili, Sufi shaykhs turned to Persian verse more so than earlier mystics. The majority of them were practitioners of poetry. Some of them, like Shaykh Safioddin himself or Shâh Dâ'i Shirâzi in *Kân-e malâhat* [Mine of Tenderness], composed poetry even in local dialects, the dominant and most popular poetic form being the *ghazal*. Other verse forms such as *qasideh*, *tarji'band*, and quatrains are infrequently seen; and except for rare instances such as the strophic poem of Hâtef (d. 1720),[27] they usually have little literary merit. In general, Sufi verse and prose of this period failed to reach the level attained in the Classical period: neither the thought nor the feeling was at that former level, nor was the language, the medium of expression. As stated earlier, among the twelve masters of Persian prose of the nineteenth century listed by Âryanpur, eleven were members of the court or government administration. Not only was none of them a religious scholar, but no one on the list was a Sufi either.[28] No trace remained of the past richness of mystical prose.

The Law and the Way: Difference in Language

Between the prose of religious scholars and that of mystics a substantial and fundamental difference exists, not in the period of decline, but rather in the age of the blossoming of thought and expression. The language of these two sources of prose differs because their subjects are not the same. Religious law treats the commonest basic problems

---

27. E.G. Browne, *A Literary History of Persia*, Vol. 4 (Cambridge University Press, 1959, first published 1924) presents a text and translation of Hâtef's poem, pp. 284–97.

28. Âryanpur, *From Sabâ to Nimâ*.

and daily duties in life even when the law is not dealing with transactions and contracts and cleansing, but rather with supernatural matters and with worship; for example, in addressing prayer. The law focuses on the conditions, the rules, and the prescriptions for carrying out duties and not the readiness of the heart and the spiritual state of the person praying and his relation with his origin, because the nature of such things, even if amenable to discussion, is not the business of religious law. Or, for instance, concerning the hajj pilgrimage, religious prose treats ceremonies and practical aspects such as ritual purity, the run between Safa and Marwa and other prescribed activities, not the interior and uplifting meaning of this pilgrimage.

Religious law focuses on the regulations that are conduits for the execution of Islamic duties, those aspects which bring religion down from the spiritual world to the level of mundane actions. It deals with ordinary and fixed matters and busies itself with setting the boundaries for these matters. Its duty begins from the moment religion descends from heaven to earth. Consequently, the subject of its prose is earthbound and not conducive to flight.

In contrast, Sufi discourse is skybound and soars, because the Sufi Way begins at that very place where earthly man desires another place and condition. The subject of the Way is the journey and behavior of humankind, the interior journey of Everyman, who sets out from his abode for unknown caravan stops beyond, on the other side of fixed and accessible boundaries. Mystical experience is personal, exalted, and transforming. The language of mysticism expresses the difficulties of this experience, the experience of this state. Mysticism speaks of a matter and state conditionally passing and behavior of an internal experience that does not stand still. Consequently the language must soar, must strive continually upward.

Having mentioned prayer and the language of religious law, I might also cite the prayer of the entranced gnostic 'Aynolqozât, lost to self and consumed by love, who put his soul into words. In his opinion, prayer is not a matter of the habit of worship, because "the way of men who have smashed the idols of habit is other than the way of the effeminate and unmanly and would-bes who make the idol of habit the object of their worship . . . If being on the path of [his] fathers was necessary and proper, Abraham was on the path of fire . . . What do you think, that prayer is easy, that prayer is rising out of habit and genuflecting out of habit and prostrating oneself out of habit? Never! . . . One of the signs of love is excessive mention of the beloved and prayer is mention of the beloved."[29] 'Aynolqozât treats the pillars of prayer in twenty-six letters. But he does not speak merely of regulations and rules of the Law. The speaker talks of the forlorn state of Satan, knowledge, divine attributes, events and acts, faith, divine knowledge, his love and enmity and other things, "that of which his lonely heart wants to speak."

Religious law specifies the subject of language with set formulas and rules. A subject of such clarity and explicitness forces its own characteristics on its language also. When discussing an experiential body of knowledge, one must perforce speak with the language of that science, pruning any extra branches and leaves. Religious law likewise sets the limits for its language, and the language encompasses the subject (because both become coterminous).

But in the Sufi path, the subject is not a matter situated in the external world or an external phenomenon, but rather a personal and fleeting experience. Here the subject of discourse constantly pulls language along, giving it no opportunity to remain static. This language is perforce exalted and leaves its boundaries behind. As a result of this constant movement of thought and discourse, the speech of gnosticism is sometimes complex, contrary to customary logic, paradoxical, or, to use their own expression, *shat'h,* "ecstatic." The prominent twelfth-century mystic Ruzbehân Baqli says: "Ecstatic utterance is movement, and the house in which they grind flour, they call the "ecstasy-mill" because of the amount of movement in it. Therefore in the speech of Sufis ecstatic utterances stem from the motions of the secrets of their heart . . . When they see visions and things of the unseen and the secrets of grandeur, intoxication comes upon them involuntarily, their souls are agitated, secrets boil over, they begin to talk . . ." Ruzbehân's *The Exposition of Ecstatic Utterances,* which deals mainly with the unraveling of secrets of utterances of Bâyazid Bestâmi (d. 874), "the Sultan of Gnostics," and Hosayn b. Mansur Hallâj (d. 872), "the Shah of the Birds of Love," is perhaps the example par excellence in Persian prose of the movement and dynamism of classic mystical language, a language which sometimes tries with great effort to parallel the speedy and hasty movement of thought and state, a language racing within itself and

---

29. 'Aynolqozât, *Nâmeh'hâ-ye 'Aynolqozât-e Hamadâni* [Letters of 'Aynolqozât of Hamadân], 2 vols., edited by 'Alinaqi Monzavi and 'Afif 'Osirân (Tehran: Bonyâd-e Farhang-e Irân, 1969) 1: 225, 262; 2: 20.

passing beyond itself, the language of the mystic wayfarer. In poetry, perhaps Rumi's *Divân-e Kabir* [Collected Poems] is the best example.

Besides, on the subject of speech of gnosticism, the moment a writer or composer wants to express a passing and impermanent state, he makes it permanent in discourse. A fluid matter is transformed into a fixed condition and as a result appears in a different guise, becomes something else. Perhaps because of this, gnostics continually complain about the ineloquence of language. They feel the need of "lacerated breast" to give a clue to the condition of their souls. Essentially, gnosticism is a matter of "secrets." Gnostic knowledge and attainment of divine truth, although they may have set customs and formalities, must inspire the gnostic's heart. It does not come with study of science, it is a task of discovery and observing. The gnostic is witness to a secret not only are others unaware but which also is indescribable. It won't fit within the confines of discourse. Speaking about such a perception of truth, or better, of divine truth, is naturally very difficult because the prior conception of such a perception is that the place and abode of divine truth is beyond the world of language.

In contrast, the language of religious law does not face a special problem in expressing its meaning. For this reason it has no need for metaphor, allusion, imagery, symbol and other formal means and instruments. It has at hand its thesaurus of words. It suffices that one use each word with its literal denotation to put across its point. On the other hand, for reasons already stated the language of the Sufi path needs to utilize all of these means and enter into other dimensions and areas of language to provide an intimation of an indescribable state. The language of Sufism is necessarily figurative and symbolic. A look at the prose of 'Attâr, Sohravardi, 'Aynolqozât and Nasafi shows that love, unity, cupbearer, wine, goblet, beloved, faces, mirrors, intoxication, madness, Simurgh, the world of exile, the world of semblances, illumination, intuitive witnessing, manifestation . . . and many other concepts and terms with which anyone familiar with Persian literature is acquainted play a deep, complex, and multifaceted role in the expression of Sufi aims. These are not merely figurative expressions, symbols, and images, and the issue does not stop at the bounds of style and manner of expression. In its period of ascendancy, Sufism brought into existence "another" language, a lofty language of analogy, open and fluid, which suited a world view without boundaries. In contrast with the dry and mundane language of religious scholars which cast seeds on the ground, the language of the Sufis soared into the air, in the distant and high "path" of divine truth.

Mystic and scholar spoke not with two styles and manners, but on two disparate levels of the Persian language, on the level of state and the level of statement. In the words of 'Aynolqozât in his *Letters*: "We have a language other than this language, / A realm other than hell or heaven."

Readers will note that my presentation with respect to courtiers and clerics differed slightly from the case of the Sufis. In the case of the first two groups, I tried to sketch their cultural and social situation and to state in terms of their situation the nature of their relation, positive or negative, with national feeling and consequently with the Persian language. In the case of the third group, the presentation was more indirect. Their social locus was the same as that of religious scholars, or at least the audience of religious scholars and of Sufis were in similar situations from the social perspective, but the role of scholar and mystic was different in point of culture and language.

The nature of Islamic mysticism is incompatible with national feeling. Principles of belief and gnostic direction and behavior deal with the supernatural and concern the relation of humans with the supernatural world. Gnosticism is a "cultural-social" phenomenon, the path to salvation proposes a method in practice which is non-social and in time personal. As a result, gnosticism has nothing to do with social or historical issues, among them national matters. Iranian gnostics used the Persian language not because it was a national language, but because it was a native tongue. In fact, they did not turn to it, they were in its midst. Their link with the Persian language was not simply a matter of social-political or national stimulus or character; in the first instance it was an existential connection. Being in terms both of the context of knowledge and attainment of divine truth (a spiritual matter) and in social behavior (a practical matter) diametrically opposed to scholars of religion, the Baghdad caliphate and the governmental system, the Sufis were likewise in terms of language unsympathetic and of alien tongue.

In addition, Sufi culture differed from the cultures of religious law and government. The business of religion was in the hands of the clerics, while the business of the world was in the hands of courtiers. The members of the court dealt with mundane (not sacred) forms of culture, both in verse and in prose, in *shâhnâmeh*s, histories, wisdom literature like *Kalileh and Demneh*, and *The Rose Garden*. Sufi culture is not worldly in the court and administrative sense, and is not religious in the sense of jurisprudence, theology, Traditions, and Koranic commentaries. Whatever the definition of gnostic culture may be, it is certain that it (in its ascendancy, not in its decline) was usually in conflict with both the religious and the governmental systems. Moreover, gnostic culture turned its back on the Baghdad caliphate, which had gathered both of these within itself, and on the official representatives of religion and government. In this fashion, gnosticism took refuge indirectly and unawares in an Iranian, national and inner-bounded location, and for practical purposes, in the course of Iranian history it took the form of an asylum for the Iranian soul.

Epilogue

Discussion of the role of the courtier, the cleric, and the gnostic vis-à-vis the Persian language and Iranian nationality concludes here with a few final observations. In the context of national feeling I focused mostly on the written language—and that of prose rather than poetry—and not on language in general. In order to avoid confusing concepts, I discussed primarily the identity of national feeling, not "nationality," a term with a more recent meaning and the use of which can lead to misunderstanding if applied retrospectively.

As for this "national sentiment," it has been changeable throughout our history. It has never been a single state and with a single meaning. It was not a single state because it fluctuates in intensity. Sometimes it has been vitally present on the historical stage and instrumental in shaping and nurturing history, while at other times it has lurked like a shadow in the wings, awaiting rediscovery.

Besides its fluctuating state, "national sentiment" is subject to vacillations of meaning as well. National sentiment in the age of the Samanids and others in the tenth century differed from national sentiment at the beginning of the Safavid era in the sixteenth century, both in inspiration and aim. Put in other terms, a distinctive character and personality has shaped each period of Iranian history. By shape I mean not just visible form, but something similar to pattern, that form which necessarily becomes manifest in the internal composition of the motive factors of a phenomenon. Thus, in the study of any period one must search for distinctive characteristics of that period which will highlight differences in perception and, in some circumstances, even differences in research methodology.

What may be said about the distinctive characteristics of one period, for example the building of national sentiment on the twin pillars of language and history and the connection of language with history and awareness in the tenth century, does not hold in another age, for example, the Qajar, when language, history and awareness have a different relationship with one another and with national sentiment. In the national politics of the Safavids, as opposed to the Samanids, language played no role since they had no affection for Persian. The religious politics of the Buyids and Shi'i Safavids and the role of religion in the establishment of the state and the continuation of their government were very different.

Perhaps the above seems to belabor the obvious. But I have alluded to these self-evident matters to avoid a basic error. My observations about the relationship between the Persian language and Iranian national senti-ment involved an attempt to focus on an historical matter, which in turn has had and continues to have its own history, which is to say, development and change. In this fashion, both the phenomenon of language and the phenomenon of nationality, especially after the Constitutional period (1905–1911), developed a totally new meaning and today play a different role in our social life.

In past ages the Persian language brought into being a literature and a culture which linked and brought together all non-Persian speaking peoples in Iranian lands. The atmosphere of this culture nurtured the souls of those who spoke other languages or dialects as well. In our twentieth-century age, the meaning of language and especially local languages and their connection with nationality has changed, as has the very notion of nationality. Moreover, the issue of nationality must be seen and studied in relation to other peoples, not only immediate neighbors but also in distant world powers, because of the significance of relations and mutual influence in this sphere. I have strayed a bit from the main argument so that the focus on history might not lead to error concerning the present age.

This study has not pursued the subject of nationality and language beyond the beginning of the twentieth century, that is to say, from the Constitutional Revolution. The Constitution was a turning point in the history of Iranian society. From that time forth, together with and as a result of other developments, the cultural roles of various social classes and groups also changed. Of course these classes and groups could not remain in their pristine state, but became something else. How the social change took place, however, is not the business of our discussion. What is important is that changes in the role of social groups and in the structure and societal role of the government resulted in an end to courtiers in their previous form. Courtiers relinquished their places to employees of governmental organizations who had different cultural training, had learned different things, and had come onto the scene for a different task. They were not necessarily men of letters, and language did not constitute the basis of their education. In the complex and varied system of a nation-state, various sorts of knowledge were necessary which superceded belles-lettres. As a result, courtiers were no longer courtiers, but rather government employees. Precisely for this reason they no longer had a mission with respect to language. Their work had been finished. Likewise, Islamic mysticism, which had been living in a state of intellectual torpor for several centuries, losing its creativity both as a concept and a culture-building mode of life, no longer had anything new to say either in the world of thought or in the realm of language.

Our contact with the West, the influx of a new civilization and . . . in short those very factors that caused the disappearance of literate courtiers also destroyed Sufi gnosticism as a way of life influential in culture and language. In place of these two groups, just before the Constitutional Revolution another group appeared on the scene with a sense of responsibility toward the Persian language: literary intellectuals and writers. For nearly a century they have shouldered the burden of nurturing Iranian nationality and the Persian language. One can only hope that they prove capable of leading the Persian language to its next stage and that the fate of this language and the people who speak it is better tomorrow than it is today.

Lightning Source UK Ltd.
Milton Keynes UK
UKOW02f0832031215

263947UK00003B/116/P